ONE LORD, ONE FAITH, ONE BAPTISM, ALL YOUR QUESTIONS ANSWERED WITH SCRIPTURES

Elijah Paul

Elijah Paul Ministry

Copyright © 2024 Elijah Paul Ministry

All rights reserved

No part of this book may be reproduced, or stored in a retrieval system, or transmitted in any form or by any means, electronic, mechanical, photocopying, recording, or otherwise, without express written permission of the publisher.

ISBN-13: 9798987467527

Cover design by: Art Painter
Library of Congress Control Number: 2018675309
Printed in the United States of America

CONTENTS

Title Page

Copyright

Foreword

Failing to Be Baptized Properly Could Bring Damnation to Your Soul	1
Repentance	2
Why Are There So Many Different Forms of Baptisms?	3
Why Do Some People Say That We Are Not Required to Be Baptized?	4
A List of the Many Things That Were Done in the Name of the Lord	6
Many Ministers Do Not Baptize in the Name of the Father, and of the Son, and of the Holy Spirit	9
The "Trinity" is Not in the Bible, So Where Did It Come From?	11
This Is Why People Learned to Baptize in the Name of a Manmade Trinity	13
Rejection of the Baptism in Christ's Name is Antichrist	18
The First Baptism in History	20
The Apostles Only Baptized in Christ's Name	22
Christ Gave the Apostles More Authority Than Any Preacher	28

There Is Only One Church, One Foundation & One Body of Christ	30
Preventing People from Being Baptized in Christ's Name is Anti-Christ	32
Brides Take the Name of Grooms & Proper Baptism Gives us Christ's Name	34
Christ's Name Is Above Every Name in Heaven, Earth, & Hell	36
God the Father, God the Son, God the Holy Ghost Were in Christ, Being One	37
Father, Son, and Holy Ghost Are Titles, Not Names	39
This Is Why the Father, Son & Holy Ghost Are One	40
The Baby Jesus Was Called Father and God	45
We Must Be Born Again of the Water & of the Spirit to Go to Heaven	46
Father, Son & Holy Ghost Have the Same Name	47
What Happens to Infants & People Who Cannot be Baptized?	51
We Are Born in Sin, but Aren't Babies Born Innocent?	54
Children and Baptism	56
Christ Is Holy and Sanctified Like We Should Be	58
People Who Do Not Obey the Apostles' Doctrine Are Spiritually Blind	59
Why Does God Work in Three Revelations & Manifestations of Himself?	60
Christ & God Are One, So What Happened to Christ's Human Body After He Went to Heaven?	63
"Let Us Make Man in Our Own Image," Was Spoken to Who?	69
What Is the Name of the Father, Son, and Holy Spirit?	74
Confessing with Your Mouth, Believing in Your Heart, and	79

Calling on the Name of the Lord	
Believing and Confessing, and Accepting the Lord's Supper Unworthily	80
We Must Live Holy in This Present World	81
Broken Promises to God Make Life Worse Than Before	82
Living in the Flesh is War Against the Body & Soul	83
Some People Believe & Confess but Are Full of the Devil	85
Confessing Christ While Being an Oppressor & High-Minded	87
Fearing God Causes Forgiveness	88
Faith Without Works is Dead & Believing Without Obeying Is Dead	92
Being Too Stubborn or Too Sick to Call on the Lord	93
Grace Does Not Mean That We Should Be a Slave to Sin	95
Obedience Is Better Than Sacrifice	97
Satan Believes and Confesses but Satan also Fears God	98
The Devil Is the Father of Habitual, Rebellious and Willful Sinners	99
God Tests the Heart, So Be Careful How You Claim to Have a Good Heart	100
What Is in Your Heart Will Come Out	103
We Must Suffer like Christ & Not like a Sinner	105
Some People Go to Hell After Believing, Confessing & Calling on Christ	108
We Must Be Christ – like on Earth to Be Like Christ in Heaven	111
God Does Not Hear the Prayers, Calls & Crying of Some People	112
It Will Be Too Late to Call on God on Judgment Day	115
Christ is Ashamed of People Who Are Ashamed to Cry Out	116

unto Him	
Your Heart Shall Be Where Your Values Are	117
Some People Do Not Cry Out to God Because of Fear of Losing Human Favor	118
Ask God What Else That He Wants You to Do	120
We Must Repent & Live a Holy & Sanctified Life	121
Believing, Confessing & Calling on God Must Include Baptism	125
Blessings Do Not Always Mean That a Person is Saved	133
Obeying Only Three Verses of the Bible Does Not Save You	135
Confessing with Your Mouth, Believing in Your Heart	136
BONUS READINg	139
Coronavirus (COVID-19)	140
References	145
About The Author	147
Books By This Author	149
Back Cover Summary	151

FOREWORD

More and more ministers are falsely teaching that people do not need to be baptized at all to become a born-again Christian. This book peacefully explains with supporting Holy Scriptures how God is One Lord, and that God's plan is for there to be only One Faith, meaning one church. The name of the church does not matter if the church members are on the one foundation of God, and part of the one body of Christ. It is still acceptable to identify a church as, for example, the Methodist Church, the Catholic Church, or the Baptist Church, but there is only one foundation, One Faith, and truthfully One Baptism that is ordained by God Almighty. This book also explains how, "Confessing with Your Mouth, Believing in Your Heart, and Calling on the Name of the Lord" is vital in the life of a Christian, but this is not all that must be done to become a born-again Christian. There is one Bonus Reading titled, "Coronavirus (COVID-19)." This is the fifth book published by the author Elijah Paul and it is a Holy Ghost given guide to becoming a saved, born-again Christian, and a new creation in Christ.

FAILING TO BE BAPTIZED PROPERLY COULD BRING DAMNATION TO YOUR SOUL

Baptism is to wash away sins by being immersed in water, signifying the death, burial, and resurrection of Christ (Rom. 6:1–5; Col. 2:12; 2 Tim. 2:11).

To bury your sins in water while you rise out of the water to newness of life, becoming a born-again Christian, a new creature, and new creation (John 3:3–7; Rom. 8:5–14; 2 Cor. 5:17; 1 Pet. 1:23).

The Bible says that soap and water cannot wash away our sins (Jer. 2:22; Matt. 23:27–28). But the Spirit of Christ, the blood of Christ, and water together washes away our sins, and the Bible says that these three agree as one (1 John 5:6–8). We must also allow Christ to give us the Spirit of the Holy Ghost, also called the Holy Spirit. Because Christ says we must be born again of the water and of the Spirit, or we cannot go to heaven (Acts 2:36–39; 8:14–17; 10:42–48; 19:1–6; John 3:3–7; Mark 16:16; Rev. 21:8, 27; 22:14–15).

REPENTANCE

We should repent while being baptized. We get baptized to try to go to heaven, not only for healing, earthly possessions, or problem-solving. These things will be added at some point in your sanctified life, and they are sometimes added immediately after baptism (Matt. 6:31–34). When we truly repent, we repent unto life (Acts 11:18). Because godly sorrow causes repentance unto salvation, but worldly sorrow causes death (2 Cor. 7:9–10; Ps. 38:15–18; 85:8; Ezek. 18:21–22).

Therefore, true repentance gives us life everlasting in heaven (Gal. 6:7–8; Matt. 19:29; Luke 14:26–27; 18:29–30; Deut. 33:9).

Jesus preached repentance while he was on Earth and after he went back to heaven when he revealed himself to John. He says that he gave certain people time to repent, but they did not repent and that they will be punished with great tribulation and death unless they repent (Rev. 2:19–23).

WHY ARE THERE SO MANY DIFFERENT FORMS OF BAPTISMS?

Baptism in water has become a very controversial subject, but it should not be, because God is not the author of confusion (1 Cor. 14:33; Heb. 6:1–6). There is one Lord, one faith, one baptism (Eph. 4:4–6). So, why do Christians have so many ways of baptizing? All methods of baptism do not mean the same, because the Bible says that there is only one baptism (Eph. 4:4–6). Some people baptize in the name of the Lord Jesus Christ, some people sprinkle water, some people pour water, some people baptize in the name of the Father, and of the Son, and of the Holy Ghost, and some people say we do not need to be baptized at all to be saved. We should speak the same thing, have the same mind, and the same judgment, without division (1 Cor. 1:10).

There is only one interpretation of God's Word. Two people cannot have two different interpretations of the Word of God (2 Pet. 1:20; 1 Cor. 14:36). You are either right or wrong, because the Word of God is of no private interpretation, and it is not revealed to only one person (2 Pet. 1:20; 1 Cor. 14:36).

Considering that there is only one baptism, then sprinkling (aspersion), and pouring (affusion), it is not right, because it is not enough water to cover the whole body. Thus, all sins are not washed away, and you may not be filled with the Holy Spirit. The Spirit, water, and blood agree as one (1 John 5:6–8). Also, sprinkling and pouring is not in the Bible.

WHY DO SOME PEOPLE SAY THAT WE ARE NOT REQUIRED TO BE BAPTIZED?

A preacher once said, and many inaccurate preachers since that time have said, that we do not need to be baptized in water at all because the Bible according to him says we are baptized in the blood of Jesus and not in water. But as stated before, the Bible says the blood and water agree as one (1 John 5:6–8). Heb. 10:22 says, "Let us draw near God with a pure heart in full assurance of faith…and having our bodies washed with pure water." And yes, the Bible says that we are washed by the blood of Jesus Christ, but the Bible also says that we are washed by water and that the Spirit, water, and blood agree as one (1 John 5:6–8; Rev. 1:5; 7:14).

John the Baptist baptized a multitude of people including Jesus, and Peter and the apostles baptized three thousand people in one day during the first ever baptism after the resurrection of Christ (Matt. 3; Acts 2:36–47). John the Baptist refused to baptize Jesus because he felt that he was not worthy to baptize Jesus, but Jesus told John the Baptist that he must baptize him to fulfill all righteousness (Matt. 3). Therefore, to be baptized in water is right, and it is ordained by God. If being immersed in water is not important, why was John the Baptist baptizing people in the Jordan River (Matt. 3:1–6)? If sprinkling and pouring is right, why did John go to the town of Aenon to baptize people? The

Bible says that John baptized people in the town of Aenon because there was plenty of water there (John 3:23). Why did Philip baptize the eunuch in water (Acts 8:38)? Notice the preacher got in the water with the person who was being baptized (Acts 8:38). The preacher did not send someone else into the water to do the baptizing for him while he prayed from outside of the water, like some preachers do nowadays. Why did Jesus himself get fully immersed in water (Mark 1:9–10)? Are we not all supposed to do everything like Jesus did? Some people nowadays say that baptizing in water puts too much emphasis on ceremonial means. But Jesus says that if you do not believe and get baptized as he and the apostles did, you shall be damned (Mark 16:16; Acts 2:38; 8:14–17; 10:47–48; 19:2–5; John 3:3–7; Rev. 21:8, 27; 22:14–15).

Most preachers who do not believe in baptism have large churches and do not want to take the time to baptize all their people. If getting wet is a problem for the minister, he can wear a waterproof suit. Why didn't the apostles baptize by sprinkling and pouring but instead baptized everyone by getting in the water with them, and fully immersing the new believer in water and raising them back up out of the water (Acts 2:38; 8:14–17; 10:47–48; 19:2–5)?

A LIST OF THE MANY THINGS THAT WERE DONE IN THE NAME OF THE LORD

Colossians 3:17 commands us to do all things in the name of Jesus, whether it is in word or deed. We preach in Christ's name (Luke 24:47; Acts 9:27–29). We speak in the name of the Lord (James 5:10). We preach in the name of the Lord (Jer. 26:11, 16). We teach in Christ's name (Acts 4:16–20). And the apostles were forbidden and nearly killed for teaching in Christ's name (Acts 4:28, 33). We command in Christ's name (2 Thess. 3:6). We cast out devils, do miracles, and give to others in Christ's name (Mark 9:38–41; Acts 16:16–18; Heb. 6:10).

The devil is subjected unto us through Christ's name (Luke 10:17). We receive children in Christ's name (Mark 9:37). We ask the Father for things in Christ's name (John 16:23–24). We ask God for healing in Christ's name (Acts 3:1–6, 12, 16). We give thanks in Christ's name (Eph. 5:20). We anoint and pray for the sick in Christ's name (James 5:13–15). Our help is in the name of the Lord (Ps. 124:8). We even suffer for the sake of righteousness in the name of Christ (Acts 5:38–42). We are washed, sanctified, and justified in the name of Jesus, but by the Spirit of God. It is that same one Spirit but a new name (1 Cor. 6:9–11).

We are supposed to celebrate Christmas in Christ's name, but the love of the world and the love of money have caused many Christians to not say Merry Christmas during the entire

Christmas season, but they instead say Happy Holidays and Seasons Greetings. Instead of saying, "It was the night before Christmas," they say, "It was the night before gifting." And instead of saying, "The twelve days of Christmas," they instead say, "The twelve days of gifting." Instead of continuing to say Christmas break, the world is now saying winter break. Therefore, we should be happy to be baptized in Christ's name, and to not be baptized in Christ's name is to take his name out of the baptism too, just as Christ's name has been taken out of the Christmas season by many people (John 3:3–7; Acts 2:38–39; 8:14–17; 10:47–48; 19:2–5; Rom. 8:5–14).

We lift our hands in Christ's name (Ps. 63:4). All means all (Col. 3:17). The Holy Ghost comes in the name of Jesus (John 14:25, 26). Saved people rise in the resurrection by the name of Jesus (2 Cor. 4:14; 1 Cor. 15:25, 28). Elijah built an altar in the name of the Lord when he put the prophets of Baal to shame (1 Kings 18:26–32; 19:15–18; Rom. 11:1–5).   Peter said, "Get baptized every one of you in the name of Jesus Christ for forgiveness of sins" (emphasis added) (Acts 2:38).

Again, he said every one of you, not just the Apostolic Church, Baptist, Catholic, Church of Christ, Church of God in Christ, Pentecostal, Presbyterian, or anti-Christian groups; but every one of you must be baptized in the name of Jesus Christ (Acts 2:36–39; 8:14–17; 10:42–48; 19:1–6; John 3:3–7).

Even in the Old Testament, people did things in the name of the Lord, but not in the name of the Father, because Father is a title, not a name. They blessed in the name of the Lord (2 Sam. 6:18; Deut. 10:8; 1 Chron. 23:13; Num. 6:23–27). They ministered in the name of the Lord (Deut. 18:5, 7). They walked in the name of the Lord (Mic. 4:5; John 8:31–47). They rejoiced in the name of the Lord (Ps. 89:16). Zechariah and Haggai prophesied in the name of God (Ezra 5:1). The people set up their banners in the name of the Lord (Ps. 20:5). Just as some people do not baptize in the name of the Lord, they do not bless you in the name of the Lord either (Ps. 129:8). If you do not do all these things in the name of the Lord Jesus Christ, you have limited power (Acts 3:16). Moses was not allowed to go to the promised land because he did not speak to the rock in the name of the Lord (Exod. 17:7; Num. 20:7–13; 27:14; Deut. 6:16; Ps. 106:32–33). By not speaking to the rock in the name of the Lord, Moses did not believe God and did not sanctify God in the presence of the people (Num. 20:12). The same applies when people do not believe the one baptism. When you pray, you are not going to pray to the Son or Holy Ghost, because they are titles, not names. You are going to pray to the Father, which is a title also, but in Christ's name (John 16:23–24). We pray unto the Father in the name of Christ. We start our prayers by saying "Father God," and we end our prayers by saying, "In Christ's name. Amen." To not use the name Christ is having a form of godliness but denying the power thereof, and ever learning but never able to come to the power of the truth (2 Tim. 3:5).

MANY MINISTERS DO NOT BAPTIZE IN THE NAME OF THE FATHER, AND OF THE SON, AND OF THE HOLY SPIRIT

Speaking of what Jesus and the apostles did, Christ told them in Matt. 28:19 to baptize in the name of the Father, and of the Son, and of the Holy Ghost. Why didn't they do that? Were they disobedient? In Acts 2:38, when the original apostles did it for the first time after the resurrection, they did it in the name of Jesus Christ. As a matter of fact, no one in the Bible was ever baptized in the name of the Father and of the Son and of the Holy Ghost. Every time someone in the Bible was baptized after the resurrection of Christ, they were baptized in the name of Jesus (Acts 2:36–39; 8:14–17; 10:42–48; 19:1–6; John 3:3–7).

The Apostle Paul asked, "Is Christ divided? Was Paul crucified for you? Or were you baptized in the name of Paul?" (1 Cor. 1:13). No, they were all baptized in the name of Jesus (1 Cor. 1:13). Jesus baptized no one, but the apostles did the work for him, and they all baptized people in Christ's name (John 4:2). So why are most preachers nowadays not baptizing like the apostles did in the Bible (Acts 2:36–39; 8:14–17; 10:42–48; 19:1–6; John 3:3–7)?

John the Baptist preached the baptism of repentance for the remission of sins (Mark 1:4). In Acts 2:38, Peter preached a similar sermon when he said, "Repent, and be baptized every one of you in the name of Jesus Christ for the remission of sins, and you shall receive the precious gift of the Holy Spirit." God himself says that Jesus was sent for the remission of our sins and to teach us about salvation (Luke 1:76–78). Christ purchased us with his blood, so shouldn't we be baptized in his name? But some people deny Christ who purchased them, even in baptism (1 Cor. 3:9; 6:13–20; 7:21–24; Acts 20:28; 2 Pet. 2:1–2; Deut. 32:6).

THE "TRINITY" IS NOT IN THE BIBLE, SO WHERE DID IT COME FROM?

In AD 325, the Catholic Church held its first council of Nicaea. The Council was organized by Emperor Constantine and maybe the pope. At this council, bishops, priests, and certain pagan religious leaders came together to discuss their baptisms and the trinity, among other false doctrines. This controversy began in the second century. Before that time, the word trinity was not used because it is not in the Bible. Thus, it was never used among the original apostles and apostolic followers. It was introduced by theologians of the second century to try to explain the oneness of the Father, the Son, and the Holy Spirit. The answer is in Col. 2:8–9 when the scripture says, "Beware, lest anyone spoil you through philosophy and vain deceit, after the tradition of men... For in Jesus dwells all the fullness of the Godhead bodily" (emphasis added).

And in 1 John 5:7, the scripture says, "These three are one," meaning the Father, Son, and Holy Ghost are one. Christ says that whoever receives him also receives Father God Almighty (Matt. 10:40). Arius, a deacon of Alexandria, held that the Son was subordinate to the Father. The council ruled that the Father and the Son were equal and condemned Arius and the Arians. Later, at the Council of Constantinople in 381, 150 Catholic bishops determined that the Holy Ghost would be considered a

Third Person of God. This is how mankind decided to start using the word trinity, a word that is not in the Bible.

No African nations were invited to the council where the manmade trinity was created. The baptism in the name of the Father, and of the Son, and of the Holy Ghost is a white peoples' baptism that was performed during slavery and that originated in the political institution of Christianity, 325 years after the resurrection. Compare that to only 50 days after the resurrection when the first baptism was performed by the black Hebrew apostles. Christianity is a white anti-Christ religion that supports slavery, oppression, sharecropping, ethnic cleansing, genocide, and Apartheid, and is opposite of the Christian Faith of Holiness and Sanctification (James 3:17 – 18; Isa. 61:1 – 3; Luke 4:16 - 21; James 1:26 – 27; 1 Tim. 1:8 – 10; Heb. 2:11; 12:14; Exod. 21:16; 23:9; Lev. 25:14, 17; Deut. 23:15 – 16; 24:7; 1 Peter 1:16).

THIS IS WHY PEOPLE LEARNED TO BAPTIZE IN THE NAME OF A MANMADE TRINITY

As with any Christian denomination, not all Catholics are bad and there are good and not so good people in every denomination. Romans changed the names of the days of the week and the names of the months of the year in honor of idol gods and goddesses. Before that, God himself named the months of the year. Roman Catholics changed the word Passover to the word Easter, which is in the King James Version of the Bible only one time and should not be. Roman Catholics apparently changed the baptism in one part of the Bible from being baptized in Christ's name to being baptized in the name of the Father, and of the Son, and of the Holy Spirit. The original apostles never baptized anyone that way, but everyone in the Bible was baptized in the name of Christ (Acts 2:36–39; 8:14–17; 10:42–48; 19:1–6; John 3:3–7).

Therefore, just as we call the first and second day of the week Sunday and Monday, for example, even though they are named for the so-called sun god and moon god, a lot of people get baptized in the name of the Father, and of the Son, and of the Holy Spirit because it is embedded in people's minds and hearts. Being baptized in the name of the Father, and of the Son, and of the Holy Spirit has become just as common and easy to do as saying Sunday and Monday although those days and all days of the week honor idol gods. But the saving of a person's soul from hell should cause people to want to be baptized correctly (John 3:3–7; Acts 2:36–39; 8:14–17; 10:42–48; 19:1–6).

Christ died for all people, so those of us who are living should no longer live for ourselves, but for Christ who died for us and rose from the dead (2 Cor. 5:15; 1 John 2:2–4; Acts 17:26; Heb. 2:9; Rom. 5:6–9; 8:32; Isa. 53; John 11:47–57; Acts 10).

As stated earlier, the Bible says that there is no private or misinterpretation of the Word of God, we are either right or wrong (2 Pet. 1:20; 1 Cor. 14:36). But there are a few mistranslations of terms in the King James Version of the Bible. Passover was replaced with Easter in Acts 12:4. Passover originated thousands of years before Easter. Passover was a holy day, while Easter was, and still is, a pagan and heathen holiday in honor of a sex goddess. Most people try to celebrate them at the same time of the year, and some Christians participate in the evil rituals. It is all right to celebrate the death, burial, and resurrection of Jesus; but the original purpose of Easter was to honor an evil goddess. Whoever added Easter to the Bible may be on their way to hell, according to the following scriptures: Rev. 22:18–20 and Deut. 4:1–4 and 12:32. Therefore, we know the term Easter should not have been put in the Bible by man, and it is possible that the baptism in the name of the Father, and of the Son, and of the Holy Ghost should not have been placed in the Bible either. Evidence of Easter being recklessly included in the King James Version of the Holy Bible is that most Bible scholars and publishers do not include it in other versions of the Bible because most people know better than to replace the word Passover with the word Easter. But most people are reckless and neglectful on a yearly basis when they celebrate Easter during Passover and on Resurrection Day even though most of them have learned better. Popes of the Catholic Church also changed the calendar from the Julian calendar that was named for Julius Caesar to the Gregorian calendar named for Pope Gregory XIII. And the customs and traditions of the holidays that were taken from pagans and heathen religions were added to Christianity by the Catholic Church, but Christianity is not the same as the Christian Faith, because Christianity has always been a political entity (Isa. 61:1 – 3; Luke 4:16 – 21; 1 Tim. 4:1 – 3; 6:9 – 10, 21; Acts 6:7; Rom. 1:5; 16:25 – 27; James 2:1 – 10; Phil. 1:27; 4:2, 22; Matt. 20:24 – 28; Gal. 3:28; Col. 3:11 – 15; Rev. 5:9; 7:9; 14:6).

Just as people are accustomed to saying Easter instead of Passover, Resurrection Day, or resurrection week, they are also accustomed to being baptized in the name of the Father, and of the Son, and of the Holy Ghost, instead of being baptized in Christ's name, the person who died for their sins (Acts 2:36–39; 8:14–17; 10:42–48; 19:1–6; John 3:3–7).

The Bible says there is one Lord, one faith, and one baptism (Eph. 4:4–6). But Acts 2:38 and Matt. 28:19 mention two different baptisms. The original apostles only baptized in Christ's name (Acts 2:36–39; 8:14–17; 10:42–48; 19:1–6; John 3:3–7).

So, it is possible that Roman Catholics put Matt. 28:19 in the Bible, but the apostles are accurate. Any church that does what popes and priests initiated and not what the apostles initiated are inaccurate (Eph. 2:20; Acts 2:36–39; 8:14–17; 10:42–48; 19:1–6; John 3:3–7).

They are trying to obey what Jesus said in Matt. 28:19, but are disobeying him, because the apostles nor anyone else in the Bible were ever baptized according to what is written in Matt. 28:19. If Roman Catholics did not put in the Bible the baptism in the name of the Father, and of the Son, and of the Holy Spirit and that Christ really did say that, it means that in the New Testament, God goes by the name of Christ. Christ says that he came in his Father's name (John 5:43; Rev. 14:1). Jesus says that the works that he does, he does them in his Father's name, because the Father is in Christ and Christ is in the Father (John 10:25, 37–38). And it was not the Son who did the works, but the Father (John 14:10). Either way, Jesus said that we will believe and keep his Word through what the apostles teach us (John 15:20; 17:20). What the apostles wrote should mean more than what Roman Catholics and popes wrote, and if Catholics indeed did write a false baptism in the Bible, then that would not be the true way. The Bible says the true way shall be evil spoken of (Acts 19:1–9; 1 Pet. 4:14; 2 Pet. 2:1–3). Jesus also told the apostles that whosoever shall not hear them are in more trouble than the people of Sodom and Gomorrah, the two cities that God destroyed because of sin (Mark 6:11). He told the apostles to teach and preach what he told them (Matt. 10:27). The apostles were eyewitnesses, and we should take heed and be mindful of them (Acts 4:32; 2 Pet. 1:16–19; 3:2; Heb. 2:3–4).

The apostles are only telling us what they saw and heard Christ do (1 John 1:1–4; Acts 1:1–3, 8, 22; 2:32; 3:14–15; 4:18–20, 33; 5:28–29, 32; 10:39–48; 13:31; 22:14–18; 26:16; Luke 1:1–4; 10:23–24; 24:34–53; 1 Cor. 9:1–2; Matt. 13:10–17).

Luke said he and the apostles were eyewitnesses from the beginning of Christ's ministry (Luke 1:1–4). They saw him alive for forty days after he rose from the dead by many infallible proofs (Acts 1:1–3; 2:32). They ate and drank with him after he rose from the dead (Acts 10:40–48; Luke 24:34–53). While eating with the apostles, Christ opened their understanding and told them that they are eyewitnesses and to go preach repentance and remission of sins in Jesus's name among all nations, beginning in Jerusalem (Luke 24:46–49). After Christ's Resurrection, the Word of God was not first taught at Nicaea, Constantinople, or Rome. The apostles saw and heard things that righteous people, prophets, and kings did not see, and Christ said that people are spiritually blind who do not obey what the original apostles wrote (Matt. 13:10–17; Luke 10:23–24; 2 Cor. 2:17; 4:2–5).

The apostles were beaten and commanded not to speak in the name of Jesus, but they still taught and preached Christ daily in the temple, in houses, and publicly (Acts 5:40–42; 20:19–27). Moses said, "I know that the Lord has sent me to do all these works, for I have not done them of my own mind" (Num. 16:28). Paul spoke similar words regarding himself (Gal. 1:10–12). Even Christ himself said that his doctrine is not his own, but God's, and that people who speak of themselves, seek their own glory;

but they who seek the glory of God is true and has no unrighteousness in them (John 7:14–18). Jesus said that he did nothing of himself, but he did only what he saw his Father do (John 5:19). And the apostles only did what they saw Christ do.

REJECTION OF THE BAPTISM IN CHRIST'S NAME IS ANTICHRIST

If we do not acknowledge the name of Christ in baptism, that omission is a version of the antichrist, because we would be saying that we do not need the name Christ. When you acknowledge the Son, you automatically have the Father (1 John 2:18, 22–23). What hinders you from being baptized properly (Acts 8:36–39; Gal. 5:7)? To be baptized in the name of Jesus, or of the name of Christ, or of the name of the Lord Jesus Christ, fulfills the Father, the Son, and the Holy Spirit (1 John 5:7). To be baptized otherwise is to reject Christ's name, being a form of the antichrist, but most people do not intend to be antichrist and do mean well when they are baptized improperly (1 John 2:18). But to be baptized in the name of the Father, and of the Son, and of the Holy Ghost does not fulfill any scripture, any prophecy, or any washing away of sins because the name "of" Christ was not mentioned (Acts 2:36–39; 8:14–17; 10:42–48; 19:1–6; John 3:3–7).

There is power in the name of Jesus, and demons tremble at the name of Christ (Luke 10:17; James 2:18–20; Mark 1:23–28; 3:9–12). So, if you really want to be saved from your sins and empowered by the Holy Ghost, which is also the Holy Spirit, to overcome any weaknesses, demons, or sinful habits, being baptized in the name of Christ gives you that power and it fulfills the Father, the Son, and the Holy Spirit (1 John 5:7). The word Christ is the European version of the Hebrew word Messiah

(Dan. 9:25–26; John 1:41; 4:25).

When people believe in Christ and are baptized, their vile, immoral, and wretched bodies become new and part of his glorious body (Eph. 2:19–22; Ps. 118:22; Matt. 21:42; 1 Pet. 2:7; Acts 4:11–12).

Christ is a tried stone, a precious cornerstone, and a sure foundation, built on the foundation of the prophets and the apostles, Christ being the chief cornerstone who holds up all the weight (Isa. 9:6–7; 28:16; Rom. 15:1–4). But people who reject the baptism in Christ's name are rejecting the cornerstone of the building of Christ and that cornerstone has now become the chief cornerstone in heaven, on earth, in hell, in our personal lives, in our families, in our schools, and even in prisons when we accept Christ fully. And how can we accept Christ fully if we refuse to be baptized in his name? The stone that the builders rejected has now become the chief cornerstone. When people reject the baptism in Christ's name, they too reject the chief cornerstone who is Christ. Nor is there salvation in any other, for there is no other name under heaven given among mankind that saves us (Acts 4:10–12; Eph. 2:20; Ps. 118:22; Matt. 21:42; 1 Pet. 2:6–7; Isa. 28:16).

God gave Christ all power in heaven, on earth, beneath the earth, and in hell and a name above all names, and that is another reason that being baptized in the name of Christ fulfills everything, including the Father, Son, and Holy Ghost (1 Cor. 15:24–28; Eph. 1:21–23; Col. 2:10; Phil. 2:9; Ps. 8; Heb. 2:5–9; John 16:15; Matt. 28:18).

THE FIRST BAPTISM IN HISTORY

Peter and John said they would not obey man more than God (Acts 4:19–20). But Catholics go to priests to ask for forgiveness, which is not necessary, but people who are not Catholic obey Catholic baptisms, putting themselves in the same jeopardy as Catholics, who now have a different Bible than what other Christians use. Once again, most Catholic people are good people, and non-Catholic people who allow non-Catholic ministers to tell them that they are saved because they simply believe, confess, and call on the Lord are equally in error as when Catholic people unnecessarily confess their sins to a priest with hopes to be forgiven by God. Jesus says, "If you keep my commandments, you shall abide in my love, even as I have kept my Father's commandments, and abide in his love" (John 15:10). And it was at Jerusalem that Peter and the apostles started the first church by baptizing three thousand people in the name of Jesus (Acts 1:4–5, 8–9; 2:38). Peter told them what Jesus commanded him to do, that repentance and forgiveness of sins should be preached in Jesus's name unto all nations. And when Peter performed the first baptism, he baptized the people in the name of the Lord Jesus Christ for the forgiveness of their sins (Luke 24:47; Matt. 28:19; Acts 2:38–39). This word had been preached and the baptism had been performed to the entire world by the apostles by AD 62, which was about thirty years after Christ went back to heaven (Col. 1:23; Acts 2:36–39; 8:14–17; 10:42–48; 19:1–6; John 3:3–7).

Thus, God visited the Gentiles to take out of them a people for his name (Acts 15:14).

THE APOSTLES ONLY BAPTIZED IN CHRIST'S NAME

Luke put everything in order (Luke 1:1). And he wrote the book of Acts where all people were baptized in Christ's name (Acts 2:36–39; 8:14–17; 10:42–48; 19:1–6; John 3:3–7).

And Jesus after going back to heaven showed John a revelation and told him to write the book of Revelation, a book most of us do not understand entirely (Rev. 1:10–19). The Apostle Paul knew a man who he could not figure out if the man was an angel or not. Paul said this man saw things in heaven that he was not allowed to talk about (2 Cor. 12:2–4). The apostles knew men and heavenly spirits like that, so they certainly knew more than we know. Who are you going to believe, them or present-day preachers? They said that they heard Jesus, saw him, and handled the Word of life with their hands (1 John 1:1–3; Phil. 2:14–16). The Word is God (John 1:1; Rev. 19:13). The apostles stood in the temple and taught the word of a sanctified life (Acts 5:20; John 17:17–19; Isa. 29:23).

Jesus is the image of the invisible God (Col. 1:15). One apostle said if you know God, you will hear their doctrine, and if you refuse to hear them, you have the spirit of error (1 John 4:6). Another apostle said if a man or an angel teaches you anything other than what the apostles taught, let it be accursed (Gal. 1:8–9). Paul said there is no other gospel than what they have taught (Gal. 1:6–9). In other words, preachers who baptize in the name of the Father, and of the Son, and of the Holy Ghost are accursed.

This does not mean that they are not good people of God, because we all serve the same God (Mal. 2:4–10), but only if we do everything in Christ's name (Col. 3:17, 23; 1 Cor. 10:31). Christ says no one comes unto the Father without going through him first and that it is impossible to honor God without honoring him. And we cannot get to Christ without following the apostles' doctrine (John 14:1, 6; 5:22–23; Matt. 10:40; Acts 4:12). There is only One God and One mediator and advocate between God and humans, and that is Jesus Christ (1 Tim. 2:5; 1 John 2:1). Christ also told the apostles that anyone who receives the apostles receives Christ and whosoever receives Christ receives the Father (Matt. 10:40). Christ told the apostles, "I am the way, the truth, and the life, and no one comes unto the Father but by me. If you know me, you know my Father also, and have seen him," (John 14:1–7). Anyone who attempts to come unto the Father other than going through Christ first, that person is a thief and a robber, (John 5:22–23, 36–38; 10:1–17, 24–29; 12:26; 14:1, 6; 18:37; Acts 4:12; 2 John 1:9).

People will die in their sins if they do not believe in Christ (John 8:21–24). For through Christ, descendants of ancient Jews and Gentiles have access by one Spirit unto the Father (Eph. 2:18). The Father sent the Son to be the Savior of the world (1 John 4:14). Although Christ had not been born into the world yet, when the Hebrews left slavery in Egypt and wandered in the wilderness, the people in the wilderness served the same God, ate the same spiritual meat, drank the same spiritual drink, and drank of the same spiritual Rock that followed them—that Rock was Christ—but God was not pleased with most of them, and they were destroyed by God (1 Cor. 3:5–17; 10:1–13). Therefore, not every Christian is a servant of the Lord, because some people only benefit from God's protection and prosperity while not standing for the Word of God (Luke 4:4; Exod. 24:7; Deut. 4:1–9; 8:3). The Bible speaks of an eloquent man, mighty in the scriptures, instructed in the way of the Lord, being fervent in the spirit, who taught diligently the things of the Lord, and spoke boldly about the baptism; but Aquila and Priscilla took him aside and taught him the way of God more accurately (Acts 18:24–26). The same thing is happening nowadays. There are good preachers in the word who do not baptize in the name of Christ, but they should allow someone to teach them more accurately so they can teach their congregation more accurately. There are also preachers who are lying hypocrites but who tell the truth in some cases. Paul did acknowledge them as prophets, but he said they needed rebuking sharply, because they ruin whole families (Titus 1:11–13). Paul said to do those things that you have learned, received, heard, and seen in him and the God of peace shall be with you (Phil. 4:9; 2 Tim. 3:10) and to teach no other doctrine (1 Tim. 1:3). He also said that God made him an example to us and that if you are otherwise minded, God will reveal Paul's doctrine to you (Phil. 3:17). Paul went on to say that his life, baptism, and ministry are a pattern to people who should hereafter believe (1 Tim. 1:16). That is because he was called to be a witness unto all people of what he had seen and heard (Acts 22:15–16; 1 John 1:1–3; Phil. 2:14–16). This is why Paul said, "Be ye followers of me, even as I also am of Christ. Remember me in all things and keep the ordinances as I delivered them to you" (1 Cor. 4:15–16; 11:1–3; Phil. 3:17).

The apostle's doctrine is our example (Phil. 3:17; 1 Thess. 1:5–7). Paul also said, "You are saved, if you keep in memory what I preached unto you, otherwise you have believed in vain" (1 Cor. 15:1–2). Christians often talk about the scripture that says we are to forget the things that are behind us and press toward the mark of the prize of the high calling of God in Christ Jesus. But they often fail to mention the following verses that say, "Let us therefore, as many as be perfect [or blameless] ... Let us walk by the same rule, let us mind the same thing" (Phil. 3:13–18). Paul also said, "The things that you have heard of me among many witnesses, the same commit to faithful people, who shall be able to teach others also" (2 Tim. 2:2). The Bible says mark people who do what the apostles did, and to do otherwise is to be an enemy of the cross of Christ (Phil. 3:16–18). It also says, "Mark people who cause divisions and offences contrary to the doctrine which ye have learned from the apostles and avoid them" (Rom. 16:17). The scripture goes on to say that people who are not on the foundation of the apostles use good words and fair speeches to deceive the hearts of simple-minded people (Rom. 16:18). The Bible says that the apostles are of God and they who know God hears them and they who are not of God hears not the original apostles. "Hereby know we the spirit of truth, and the spirit of error" (1 John 4:6). The apostles said, "Keep and hold the traditions which ye have been taught, whether by word, or our letter" (emphasis added) (2 Thess. 2:15). They also said, "God called you by our gospel" (emphasis added) (2 Thess. 2:14).

We are not called by the pope's or any Protestant preacher's doctrine. Paul said God shall judge the secrets of people by Jesus Christ and according to the gospel that Paul taught (Rom. 2:16). The Apostle John testified and wrote of the things he saw Jesus do, and we know that John's testimony is true and is more credible than the pope's, any priest, or any non-Catholic preacher (John 21:24). That which they have seen and heard they declared those things unto us (1 John 1:3). Jesus says that the apostles bear witness of him because they were with him from the beginning (John 15:27).

The Bible says that people who reject the Word of God will be destroyed but people who fear God shall be rewarded (Prov. 13:13). Jesus also says that whosoever hears the apostles, hears him, and whosoever rejects what the apostles said and did rejects Christ, and they who rejects Christ rejects God who sent Christ (Luke 10:16). Some people may say that they do not reject Christ, but if anyone refuses to be baptized in Christ's name, they are rejecting Christ, even if they do not mean to reject him. And when you teach people about Christ and they reject your wisdom, it is not you they reject, but they reject God (1 Thess. 4:3–8). Isaiah prophesized that Jesus will be despised, rejected, and acquainted with grief and sorrow (Isa. 53:3; Luke 22:39–46). Jesus was rejected in his own hometown (Luke 4:16–32; 9:51–58). Christ's own biological brothers did not believe in him at one point (John 7:1–8). Ultimately, Jesus came unto his own people including the ancient Jews, and his own people did not receive him (John 1:10–14; Acts 13:26–31; Luke 24:44–49).

Paul said that we should know the commandments that they gave us from Jesus (1 Thess. 4:2). Peter said of Paul that God gave him wisdom to write parts of the Bible and that all his writings are true, and some things are hard to be understood. But only unlearned and unstable people wrestle with Paul's teachings and other scriptures, to their own destruction (2 Pet. 3:14–17). John said that he was a witness to the documenting of the Word of God and of the testimony of Jesus Christ and of all things that he saw (Rev. 1:1–2; John 1:34). Are you going to believe some modern-day Protestant preacher, reverend, priest, or pope instead of believing the apostles who ate, drank, laughed, and cried with Christ? The apostles said that the people received the word that they taught not as if it was from man, but as it is in truth, the Word of God (1 Thess. 2:13). Paul was called to preach to the Gentiles, and he did not talk to the apostles for any instructions; he received instructions directly from Christ (Gal. 1:11–24). He went to Jerusalem after three years of working with the Gentiles, stayed only fifteen days talking to Peter, departed, and returned fourteen years later (Gal. 2:1, 2–10, 18). Without any instructions from Peter who performed the first ever baptism in Christ's name, Paul still preached that people should be baptized in the name of Jesus without Peter telling him to do so (Acts 19:1–6).

The Bible teaches us to withdraw ourselves from anyone who does not obey the apostles' doctrine and who does not teach their tradition (2 Thess. 3:6–7). According to the Bible, people who do not understand the apostles' doctrine are possibly blind and lost, and the apostles said that they did not handle the Word of God deceitfully, nor did they corrupt the Word of God (2 Cor. 2:17; 4:2–5; Matt. 13:10–17; Luke 10:23–24). Jesus commanded the apostles on what to do after his departure, just as Moses commanded Joshua. Joshua left nothing undone of all that the Lord commanded Moses, but people were disobedient (Josh. 11:15; Deut. 34:9). Just as most people do not follow what Jesus commanded Peter to do, and that is to baptize everyone in Christ's name (Acts 2:36–42; Matt. 16:18).

CHRIST GAVE THE APOSTLES MORE AUTHORITY THAN ANY PREACHER

Jesus told the apostles that whosoever sins they forgive, let it be forgiven, but whosoever sins they retain, let it be retained unto them (John 20:22–23). That is because Christ gave them the keys to heaven, the keys being the Word of God. Christ told Peter, "Upon this rock I will build my church, and the gates of hell shall not prevail against it. Whatever you bind on earth shall also be bound in heaven, and whatever you set free on earth shall be free in heaven" (Matt. 16:18–19). When we obey the apostles, we are freed from sin, but if we disobey the apostles, we are bound to sin and hell unless we repent (Matt. 16:18–19). And the Word of God will never be bound (2 Tim. 2:9). "Upon this rock I will build my church," Peter accepted that authority and started the first church by baptizing three thousand people in the name of Jesus and they stayed in the apostles' doctrine (Acts 2:36–42; Matt. 16:18).

When Peter started the first church and baptized the first people of the church, he spoke these words, "Repent and be baptized, every one of you, in the name of Jesus Christ for the remission of sins, and you shall receive the gift of the Holy Ghost." That is your key to the gates of heaven and the gates of hell cannot prevail against it (Matt. 16:18; Acts 2:38; John 3:3–7). If we do not deny the name of Jesus and keep his Word, the door to heaven will be open, even if you have only a little strength, but Christ will say to hypocrites, "Depart from me, you worker of iniquity" (Matt. 7:21–23; Mic. 3:11; Luke 13:24–27).

THERE IS ONLY ONE CHURCH, ONE FOUNDATION & ONE BODY OF CHRIST

The baptism in Christ's name that Peter performed on the day of Pentecost is the rock that people are rejecting and disallowing (Acts 4:10–12; Eph. 2:20; Ps. 118:22; Matt. 21:42; 1 Pet. 2:6–7; Isa. 28:16).

And people who accept the baptism in Christ's name allow Christ to be the chief cornerstone and pillar in their life, holding up their entire life (Matt. 16:18; 1 Pet. 2:6–8; Acts 2:36–39; 8:14–17; 10:42–48; 19:1–6; John 3:3–7).

God says, "I lay in Zion a chief cornerstone, elect and precious, and they who believes in him will by no means be put to shame. Therefore, to you who believe, he is precious, but to they who are disobedient, the stone which the builders rejected has become the chief cornerstone, and a stone of stumbling and a rock of offense." They stumble, being disobedient to the Word (1 Pet. 2:6–8; Luke 4:4; Exod. 24:7; Deut. 4:1–9; 8:3).

There is only one church in the entire world, and it is the one that the apostles established when Peter and the apostles baptized three thousand people in Christ's name in one day (Acts 2:36–39; 8:14–17; 10:42–48; 19:1–6; John 3:3–7).

It does not really matter what the name of a church is, but the church must be based on the apostles' doctrine, according to what Christ tells us (John 14:1, 6; 5:22–23; Matt. 10:40; Acts

4:12).

The church is the one body and foundation of Christ, and we cannot join the body of Christ or get on the foundation of Christ without being baptized in his name, and without becoming Christ's bride, but we cannot become his bride without being baptized in his name (Matt. 9:15; 2 Cor. 11:2–3; Eph. 5:23, 27; John 3:3–7; Acts 2:36–39; 8:14–17; 10:42–48; 19:1–6).

There is only one body and one foundation. "Therefore, thus says the Lord God, behold, I lay in Zion for a foundation a stone, a tried stone, a precious corner stone, a sure foundation" (Isa. 28:16). Another foundation can no one lay than what is already laid by Jesus Christ and the apostles (1 Cor. 3:11). We must all be on that same one foundation and part of that same one body of Christ. And the foundation of God stands sure, having this "seal," them who are his. "Let everyone who names the name of Christ depart from sin" (2 Tim. 2:19; 2 Cor. 1:21, 22; Eph. 1:13; 4:30).

God also uses a "seal" to identify his people in the book of Revelation (Rev. 7:4; 9:4). There is only one Spirit, one foundation, one body, one God and Father of all, who is above all, one Lord, one faith, and one baptism (Eph. 4:4–6).

PREVENTING PEOPLE FROM BEING BAPTIZED IN CHRIST'S NAME IS ANTI-CHRIST

People sometimes say that they will run on in Christ's name, but it is best to also be baptized in Christ's name if you plan to run for Christ in his name. Christ says, "Do not fear any of the things you are about to suffer. The devil will even throw some of you in prison to test you. Be faithful until death, and I will give you the crown of life" (Rev. 2:10). Paul, while in prison, was faithful until death and believed until he was executed that he would be set free (2 Tim. 4:9–18). The name of Christ is the door, and Christ says that his people will not follow another person or another god (John 10:7–9). And denying his name causes the door to close shut (Matt. 7:21–23; Mic. 3:11; Luke 13:24–27).

A good example is when Jesus spoke to the hypocrite lawyers about the persecution and killing of the prophets (Luke 11:46–52). He told them, "You have taken away the key to knowledge. You did not enter in yourself and hindered other people from entering" (Luke 11:52). The same applies to people who do not allow others to be baptized in Christ's name. Some pastors have learned better and know that the baptism in Christ's name is the one and only true baptism, one Lord, one faith, one baptism, one Spirit, one body, one hope, and one God (Eph. 4:4–6). But they refuse to teach this true way to their congregation because they fear being rejected and that the people will resist change.

BRIDES TAKE THE NAME OF GROOMS & PROPER BAPTISM GIVES US CHRIST'S NAME

When we are baptized, we become a bride of Christ. But brides are supposed to take the name of the person they have married (Rev. 19:7; 21:2; 22:17; Isa. 54:4–10; Jer. 31:27–37; Matt. 9:15; 25:1; John 3:29; 2 Cor. 11:2–3; Eph. 5:23).

When we backslide, or deny Christ's name, fail to stand for the Word of God, refuse to stand with Christ, or are ashamed of the Word of God in the presence of others, the Bible says that is the same as Christ's bride playing the role of a whore (Jer. 3:6–15, 22; Hosea 1:2; 4:15–16; 14:4–6).

Jesus says that he is coming back for people with his name (Rev. 22:4). The following scriptures are additional scriptures that say when we are baptized in Christ's name, we become married to Christ (2 Cor. 11:2; Jer. 3:14; 31:32; Isa. 62:4–5).

How can you be married to someone without having their name? When people are born into this world, they should take their earthly father's last name (Gen. 48:15–16). When we get baptized, we should become born again and accept our heavenly Father's name. You do this by getting baptized in his name, which is Christ, and by receiving the Holy Ghost (John 3:3–7;

Acts 2:36–42; 8:14–17; 10:47–48; 19:2–5).

When we receive Jesus and believe in his name, we have the power to become the sons and daughters of God (John 1:12). How can you become his son or daughter without having his name. Unless someone thinks that it is possible to be a bastard child of God. We know that it is impossible to be a bastard child of God. We are either a child of God, or a child of the devil (John 8:36–45; Mic. 4:5; 1 Tim. 5:15). And we know that being baptized in Christ's name causes even people who were born out of wedlock to no longer be a bastard (Heb. 12:4–8).

CHRIST'S NAME IS ABOVE EVERY NAME IN HEAVEN, EARTH, & HELL

Jesus has a name above every name that is named, in this world and in the world to come (Eph. 1:21; Phil. 2:9). Christ's name is above the name of any angel, even the great ones like Michael and Gabriel (Heb. 1:4–5). Every knee shall bow at the name of Christ (Phil. 2:10). His name is above any form of Jehovah, Yahweh, Allah, Muhammad, Buddha, pope, priest, father, rabbi, elder, bishop, monk, or reverend. His name is far above all principalities, dominions, and powers. He is head over all things (Eph. 1:20–22). And all judgment is now in the hands of Christ and not in the hands of God so that everyone should honor the Son of God (John 5:20–27). This is another reason that we should do all things in Christ's name (Col. 3:17). Christ says, "Everything that the Father has is mine" (John 16:15). Even hell belongs to Christ. Jesus has the keys to hell and death, and just as Satan will not work against himself, he will not build a hell for himself either (Rev. 1:18; 20:10; Luke 17:19–26; Matt. 12:22–28).

In Matt. 28:18, Jesus says that he has all power in his hands. Does this mean that God is now weak? When Christ's name became a name above all names, did God give him a name above his own? No, because they have the same name in the New Testament (John 5:43; 10:22–33). Nor is there salvation in any other name (Acts 4:12; 1 Tim. 2:5; 1 John 2:1; John 5:20–27).

GOD THE FATHER, GOD THE SON, GOD THE HOLY GHOST WERE IN CHRIST, BEING ONE

The apostles baptized in Christ's name because they knew that Jesus was telling them that the Father, Son, and Holy Ghost are the same Spirit but a different revelation of God (1 John 5:7; Acts 2:36–39; 8:14–17; 10:42–48; 19:1–6).

"There is one body and one Spirit, even as you are called in one hope. One Lord, one faith, and one baptism" (Eph. 4:4–6). How can God still be above all if he gave all power to Christ? The answer is that the Father, Son, and Holy Ghost have the same name in the New Testament and in our generations. The Bible says that there is only one Spirit, one body, one Lord, and one God and Father of all, who is above all and through all and in you all (Eph. 4:4–6; Zech. 14:9; John 5:43; 10:25; 14:26; 1 John 2:23; 5:7–8).

Therefore, the Father, Son, and Holy Ghost are the same Spirit (1 Cor. 15:24–28; Phil. 2:5–11; Ps. 8; Heb. 2:5–9; 4:12; Matt. 28:18; Rev. 1:16; 2:12–16; 19:15, 21; Eph. 1:20–23; 6:10–20; Col. 2:10; John 16:15, 21)?

Jesus was God incarnate, meaning Jesus was God in the flesh (John 1:1–14). Christ was the image of the invisible God

(Col. 1:15). God the Father, God the Son, and God the Holy Ghost were all in Jesus; and when Christ went to the wilderness to be tempted by the devil, he was full of the Holy Ghost, thus the Holy Spirit was in him (Luke 3:21–22; 4:1). But the Holy Ghost had not been given to anyone else yet (John 7:39). Christ was filled with the Holy Ghost because God was in Christ (2 Cor. 5:19). Daniel had an excellent spirit in him, but the Holy Ghost had not been given yet, so he had a good "spirit" with a lowercase "s." The same applies to Caleb who was one of two people who God allowed to go to the promised land out of thousands of people, because he had a different spirit than the other people, with a lowercase "s" (Num. 14:24). After Jesus resisted the temptation of the devil, he returned to Galilee in the "power of the Spirit," with an uppercase "S" (Luke 4:14).

FATHER, SON, AND HOLY GHOST ARE TITLES, NOT NAMES

If the Catholic Church did not write the so-called trinity in the Bible and Christ really did command us to be baptize in the name of the Father, and of the Son, and of the Holy Ghost, notice that He said name and not names. Father, Son, and Holy Ghost are titles, not names. Col. 2:8–10 tells us to beware of philosophy and traditions of humans. To baptize in the name of the Father, and of the Son, and of the Holy Ghost is simply man's tradition, because no one in the Bible ever did it (Acts 2:36–39; 8:14–17; 10:42–48; 19:1–6; John 3:3–7).

If you went to the bank and tried to deposit money into your father's and son's bank account, the banker would ask you, "What is your father's and son's name?" This is what happens when people baptize in the name of the Father and of the Son and of the Holy Ghost. They try to acknowledge, honor, and respect all three, but no name is stated. The Bible says when we acknowledge the Son's name, we automatically acknowledge the Father and the Holy Spirit, and that the Holy Spirit is sent to us in Christ's name (John 14:26; 1 John 2:23). Christ says, "I come in my Father's name, but you do not receive me. If another comes in his own name, you will receive him (John 5:43).

THIS IS WHY THE FATHER, SON & HOLY GHOST ARE ONE

Colossians 2:9 says in Jesus dwells the fullness of the godhead bodily, meaning in Jesus dwells the Father, Son, and the Holy Ghost (1 John 5:7). Just as the Father, Son, and Holy Ghost are complete in Jesus, you are complete in him if you are in his name (Col. 2:10). Father, Son, and Holy Ghost could also be a precept or short parable. Jesus often spoke in parables, and in parables, he uttered things that had been secret from the foundation of the world (Matt. 13:34–35). We know that the Spirit of God the Son was with God the Father, before the foundation of the world (Gen. 1:26; 1 Cor. 10:1–17; Ps. 66:8–12; John 17:5, 24; Heb. 1:1–2; 2 Tim. 1:9; 1 Pet. 1:20; Rev. 3:14).

David quoted by the Holy Ghost, "My Lord said to my Lord, 'Sit on my right side until I make your enemies my footstool'" (Mark 12:36). The word "Lord" is capitalized when referring to both the Father and the Son. David spoke by the Holy Ghost hundreds of years before Jesus was born. All the prophets spoke by the Holy Ghost (2 Pet. 1:20–21). Mary was pregnant by the Holy Ghost. But was not Mary pregnant by God? She was pregnant by God the Holy Ghost (Matt. 1:18). When Elisabeth was pregnant with John the Baptist, she met Mary, and the baby in Elisabeth's stomach leaped for joy while Elisabeth was being filled with the Holy Ghost. The baby leaped because God the Holy Ghost was present (Luke 1:39–44). Even John's father was filled with the Holy Ghost before the birth of Jesus (Luke 1:67). God the Father sent God the Holy Ghost in God the Son's name, and his name is Christ (John 14:26). But didn't Jesus say that he came in his Father's name (John 5:43; Luke 13:35; 19:37–38)? How can the Father send the Holy Ghost in the Son's name if the Son came in his Father's name? This is because in the New Testament, the Father, Son, and Holy Ghost come in the name of Christ, the one who suffered and paid the price to inherit all of the Father's equal authority, power, and possessions (John 16:15; 1 Cor. 15:24–28; Eph. 1:21–23; Matt. 28:18; Col. 2:10; Phil. 2:9; Ps. 8; Heb. 2:5–9; Matt. 28:18).

Christ told Father God, "I have manifested your name unto the men who you have given me out of the world... and they have kept your Word" (John 17:6). This is because the Father, Son, and Holy Ghost are one Spirit, with the same name. Christ says that whoever receives him also receives Father God Almighty (Matt. 10:40). The Bible says, "O Lord, there is none like thee, neither is there any God besides thee, according to all that we have heard with our ears" (2 Sam. 7:22; 1 Chron. 17:20). Jesus said too, "The Lord our God is One Lord" (Mark 12:29). And the people said, "Yes, he is one God, there is none other but him" (Mark 12:32). Zechariah prophesized and said that the Father shall be pierced on the cross and they shall look at the Son hanging there bleeding (Zech. 12:10). How can the Father be pierced with a spear, and it be the Son too without them being the same Spirit? The prophesy was fulfilled in John 19:34–37 and Rev. 1:7. Even before the natural birth of Jesus, the Prophet Zechariah said that God shall be one Lord and King of the Earth, and his name one (Zech. 14:9). Paul wrote of different gifts that God gives us, and the gifts come from the same Spirit, the same Lord, and the same God who works all in all (1 Cor. 12:4–6). And again, the word Spirit is capitalized, signifying God Almighty, and the scripture says that the Spirit, our Lord, and our God are the same Spirit. The Lord our God is one Lord (Deut. 6:4). The Lord is God, and there is none else (1 Kings 8:60). The Father is how God revealed himself in the Old Testament, except in the fiery furnace when the image of the Son of God appeared in the furnace with

Shadrach, Meshach, and Abed-Nego (Dan. 3:25). In the New Testament, God revealed himself as the Son, but now that Jesus has gone back to heaven, God reveals himself as the Holy Ghost, without image. When God the Son visits the earth nowadays, his visits bring destruction, wrath, chastisement, punishment, and someday soon the end of the world (1 Cor. 15:24-28; Heb. 4:12; Rev. 1:16; 2:12-16; 19:15, 21; Eph.6:10-20).

God the Holy Ghost visits the earth as the Comforter in the name of Christ, and as a protector and strengthener. And the Holy Ghost completely dwells inside of the body of righteous people (John 14:16-27; Acts 5:32; Col. 2:10). In the Old Testament, the people begged to hear Moses because if God the Father had returned, they knew they would die (Exod. 20:18, 19; Deut. 5:23-26), just as in Ezekiel's day. God used Ezekiel to warn the people before he killed them, but he did not visit the earth himself (Ezek. 3:4-21). When God walked the earth, he revealed himself as the Son. Now he reveals himself in the form of the Holy Ghost. God the Father will not be manifested again until judgment day. Then God will be all in all, and all power goes back into the Father's hand (1 Cor. 15:23-28). The Father is God in creation, the Son is God in redemption, and the Holy Ghost is the Comforter, strength, and power sent from heaven in the name of Christ, even at this present time (John 14:16-27).

When Jesus told the apostles to baptize in the name of the Father, and of the Son, and of the Holy Ghost, he was telling them to simply say Christ, or Jesus Christ, or the Lord Jesus Christ, and that covers everything, because when we acknowledge the Son, we automatically acknowledge the Father (1 John 2:22-23; Mark 9:37; Matt. 10:40). Scriptures says, "Whosoever denies the Son, the same person has not the Father, but they who acknowledge the Son has the Father also" (1 John 2:23). When God talked to Christ, Father God called the Son God, and at another time, the Son was called Lord (Heb. 1:8; Mark 12:36). God told Christ, "Your throne, O God, is forever and ever (Heb.1:8). The Bible says that this is a mystery, but that there should still be no controversy, the Bible also says that God was received up to heaven after the resurrection (1 Tim. 3:16). Jesus says that when they saw him, they were looking at the Father and that he and the Father are one (John 10:30, 38; 12:44–45; 14:6–10; 17:21–23). Christ says that whoever receives him also receives the Father (Matt. 10:40). The Apostle John said that they who abides in the doctrine of Christ, they have both the Father and the Son, and if anyone comes to you and brings not this doctrine, receive them not in your house, or you become partaker of their evil deeds (2 John 8–13). If anyone happens to hate Christ, they also hate the Father, so non-Christian religions cannot claim to love God if they do not embrace Christ (John 15:23).

A certain singer once said that the Father, Son, and Holy Ghost became one in the New Testament. But they were always one, because in John 17:5, Jesus asked God to glorify him with the glory that they had together before the world was created. Jesus was even named "Jesus" before he was conceived in Mary's womb (Luke 2:21). Isaiah 42:8 says that God will not give his glory to another. If God gave Jesus all power and a name above all names, how can Jesus not have his glory (Eph. 1:20–23)? Jesus said, "Father, glorify your name." And God said, "I have glorified it, and will glorify it again" (John 12:28). Christ told God, "Holy Father, keep through your own name the apostles who you have given me, that they may be one, as we are" (emphasis added) (John 17:11).

Jesus told God in the very next verse, "I kept them in your name" (John 17:12). Jesus tells us to ask for things in his name so the Father can be glorified in the Son. That is one reason we pray to the Father in Christ's name (John 14:13). If they had glory together before the world was created, why does Isa. 43:10–11 say that there was no God before God and that there will not be one after him? Those same scriptures tell us that God alone is our Savior because the Savior Jesus and the Savior God are the same Spirit. Again, John 14:13 tells us to ask in his name, and he will give it to us so that the Father can be glorified in the Son. Therefore, when we are baptized in Christ's name, the Father is gloried in the Son. Eph. 3:9 says that this is a mystery, which was hid in God from the beginning of the world. It goes on to say that God created all things by Jesus Christ, because they are one. God made all things through Christ, but God also says that he made all things by himself (Isa. 44:24). Christ says, "Do you not believe that I am in the Father and the Father in me? The words that I speak to you I do not speak of myself, but the Father who dwells in me does the works" (John 1:1–14; 14:10). God was in Christ (2 Cor. 5:19). Psalms 136:4 says that God alone does the wonders.

THE BABY JESUS WAS CALLED FATHER AND GOD

The Prophet Isaiah said, "Unto us a child is born, and his name shall be called Mighty God and Everlasting Father" (Isa. 9:6). If the baby was to be called Father and God, then the baby and the Father must have the same Spirit, name, and authority (Isa. 9:6). Peter tells us to be mindful of the Old Testament prophets and the commandments of the apostles (2 Pet. 3:2). We know that the world was not worthy of Jesus, but he died for us anyway (1 John 2:2–4; Acts 17:26; Heb. 2:9; Rom. 5:6–9; 8:32; Isa. 53). The Bible tells us that the world was not even worthy of the prophets and apostles (Heb. 11:36–38; James 5:5–11). So, who are you going to believe, man's doctrine or the prophets and apostles?

WE MUST BE BORN AGAIN OF THE WATER & OF THE SPIRIT TO GO TO HEAVEN

In the Old Testament, God said, "My Spirit shall not always strive with humans, because they are flesh" (Gen. 6:3). We must be born of the water and of the Spirit or we cannot go to heaven (John 3:3–7), born again, a new creature, not of the will of the flesh, blood, or mankind, but of the will of God (John 1:10–13). Because flesh and blood cannot enter heaven (John 3:3–7; 1 Cor. 15:42–52; Gal. 5:16, 24–25; 1 Thess. 4:14–17).

And they who sow to the flesh shall of the flesh reap corruption and problems, but they who sow to the Spirit shall of the Spirit reap everlasting life (Gal. 6:7–8, 14). We reap what we sow, in every aspect of life, good or bad (Rom. 2:4–11; Gal. 6:7–10).

In the Old Testament, the people served God in sincerity and truth, because the Holy Ghost had not yet been given (Josh. 24:14; 1 Sam. 12:24; 1 Kings 2:4; 3:6). But now that the Holy Ghost is a gift, we must worship God in spirit and in truth (John 4:23–24; Zech. 8:1–8).

We must compare spiritual with spiritual, because natural-thinking people cannot understand the things of the Spirit of God, because it is foolishness to them, but sanctified Christians have the mind of Christ (1 Cor. 1:10; 2:9–16; Rom. 15:5–6).

FATHER, SON & HOLY GHOST HAVE THE SAME NAME

"In the beginning was the Word, and the Word was with God, and the Word was God" (John 1:1, 14; 1 John 5:6–8; Job 27:11; Prov. 8:22–36).

Even in the New Testament, Jesus's name is called the Word of God (Rev. 19:11–13). This is because when Christ was born on earth, the Word was made flesh and dwelt among mankind (John 1:14; Heb. 2:14–15; 1 Tim. 3:16; Phil. 2:5–11; Col. 1:15).

Again, Jesus is the image of the invisible God (Col. 1:15). John the Baptist was a cousin of Jesus who was born before Jesus was born, but John said that Jesus was before him and that he did not foreknow Jesus (John 1:29–31). And John said that Christ must increase and that he and we must decrease (John 3:28, 30–31). Jesus told the ancient Jews that he was before Abraham. This proves that Jesus and God have and are the same Spirit (Eph. 2:18). Abraham was before Moses and David, but Jesus was before them all, because Jesus Christ is God's New Testament's name. Jehovah is God's Old Testament name (Exod. 6:3; Ps. 83:18). But now Christ is the name that God ordained for salvation in the New Testament, and there is no other name whereby we must be saved (Acts 4:12; John 14:4–6; 1 John 2:1).

"Thou shalt not take the name of the Lord in vain, for the Lord will not hold people guiltless who takes his name in vain" (Exod. 20:7). Jesus says that the law and the prophets of the Old Testament were preached until John the Baptist started preaching, but since that time, the kingdom of God must now be preached (Luke 16:16). Thus, in this generation, no one comes unto the Father unless they use the name Jesus and that if anyone tries to reach God in any other way, they are a thief and a robber (John 5:22–23, 36–38; 10:1–17, 24–29; 12:26; 14:1, 6; 18:37; Acts 4:12; 2 John 1:9).

Christ says we will die in our sins if we do not wear the name Christ in holiness, sanctification, and righteousness (John 8:21–24). Through Christ, descendants of the Jews and Gentiles have access by one Spirit unto the Father (Eph. 2:18). Jesus says we should honor him as we honor the Father and that if we do not honor the Son, we do not honor the Father (John 5:22–23). However, supporters of the trinity may say that they use that same scripture to honor the Father, Son, and Holy Ghost. But Jesus Christ says that he declared unto us God's name (John 17:26). Therefore, God's New Testament name is Jesus Christ. If anyone disagrees, they should tell us what name Christ was referring to when he said that he declares to us God's name and that he came in his Father's name (John 10:25; 17:26). As stated earlier, Christ says that he came in his Father's name and most people do not receive him and that when another person comes in their own name, people receive them (John 5:43). Prov. 30:4 asks, "What is God's name, and what is his Son's name?" They both are named Jesus in the New Testament because they are the same Spirit (Eph. 2:18). Jesus also says, "Anyone who believes in me, believes not in me, but in God who sent me." This means they who believe in Jesus's name believe not in Christ's name, but in the name of God (John 12:44). Christ also says that when people saw him, they saw God who sent him (John 12:45). This is one reason that the name "Immanuel" means "God with us" (Isa. 7:14; Matt. 1:23).

In the Old Testament, God revealed himself by the Holy Ghost through the prophets, but now God speaks by Jesus through the Holy Ghost in righteous teachers (2 Pet. 1:20–21; Heb. 1:1–2). God spoke to people in the Old Testament by prophets, but in these last days, God speaks to us by his Son Jesus Christ, whom he has appointed as the heir of all things, by whom God also made the entire universe (Heb. 1:8–12). God said unto the Son, "You are God," and that the Son made the heavens and the earth (Heb. 1:8–12). How is that possible? Did God make the earth? Yes, he did, but he made it with the one Spirit of the Father, Son, and Holy Ghost (1 John 5:7). Father God says, "Thus says the Lord, your Redeemer, and he who formed you from the womb. I am the Lord who makes all things, who stretches out the heavens all alone, who spreads abroad the earth by myself" (Isa. 44:24). Jesus, now being in the image of God's person, cleansed and purged us from our sins and sat on the right hand of the Majesty, meaning the right hand of royal power (Heb. 1:3). There is also a scripture that simply says, "Christ the power of God" (1 Cor. 1:24). We are baptized into Christ by one Spirit (1 Cor. 12:12–13). If Christ is one and if we are baptized into one Spirit, with a capital S, then that one Spirit is the Father, Son, and Holy Ghost all in one name. As many as have been baptized into Christ have put on Christ (Gal. 3:27; Rom. 6:3–4). There is no other way to become heirs to the promise because people who have been baptized into Christ have put on Christ (Gal. 3:26–29). How can you be baptized into Christ without being baptized in his name? How can you put on Christ without wearing his name, as in marriage (2 Cor. 11:2; Jer. 3:14; 31:32; Isa. 62:4–5)?

There is no condemnation to people who are in Christ Jesus (Rom. 8:1). Once again, how can you be in Jesus if you were not baptized in his name? Even the 144,000 virgin saints in the book of Revelation will have the Father's name written on their forehead (Rev. 14:1). And what is his name? Jesus! In Rev. 3:12, Jesus says that he will write his God's name upon us. Then he says he will write his new name upon us. God's New Testament name is Jesus, unless you think that he is going to write two different names on you. If you believe that, why didn't he say that he will also write the Holy Ghost's name on you? It is because the Father, Son, and Holy Ghost are under the same name (1 John 5:6–8). We all will have one name written on our foreheads, the name Jesus (Rev. 22:4). The Bible says in Eph.

3:14–15, "I bow my knees unto the Father of our Lord Jesus Christ, of whom the whole family in heaven and earth is named." John 14:26 tells us that God will send the Holy Ghost in Christ's name, because God, Christ, and the Holy Ghost have the same name. The Father, Word, and Holy Ghost are one (1 John 5:7). The Word was God in the beginning, and the Word became flesh (John 1:1, 14; 1 John 5:6–8; 1 Tim. 3:16).

So, God, the Word who is the Son, and the Holy Ghost are one (1 John 5:7). The word trinity is not in the Bible! Man made it up. The closest thing to trinity in the Bible is in 1 John 5:7, and it says that these three are one. Peter told the ancient Jews that they had crucified both Lord and Christ, both Father and Son (Zech. 12:10; John 19:37; Acts 2:36). The Lord our God is one Lord (Deut. 6:4). The Lord is God, and there is none else (1 Kings 8:60). Jesus said as well, The Lord our God is One Lord (Mark 12:29). And the people said, "Yes, he is one God," and that there is none other but God (Mark 12:32). After doubting the resurrection, Thomas ended up calling Jesus his Lord and his God (John 20:24–29).

WHAT HAPPENS TO INFANTS & PEOPLE WHO CANNOT BE BAPTIZED?

The Bible tells us that some people become so sick that they cannot pray for themselves and that the Spirit of God prays for them (Rom. 8:26–34). This is one way that people who are not baptized in Christ's name can go to heaven, and God will also save some people no matter how they are baptized or not baptized, because he is merciful and gracious (Rom. 8:26–34). But God's ultimate plan is for all people to be baptized in the name of his Son who died in our place (John 3:3–7; Acts 2:36–39; 8:14–17; 10:42–48; 19:1–6; Rom. 8:5–14).

Jesus was baptized by John the Baptist (Matt. 3). Some people believe that Jesus was baptized by John the Baptist for people who cannot get baptized themselves due to illness, incarceration, or isolation from the true Word of God, as in some places, or because they died as an infant. That may or may not be true, but if that is the case, everyone who is free to get baptized must do so. But people who cannot get baptized because it is beyond their control to do so, they can use the scripture that says that they are saved when they believe, confess, and call on the name of Christ (Rom. 10:9–10, 13). And in the case of babies, it does not take spiritual sense to know that babies go to heaven. Common sense tells us that. However, what some people may not understand is that it is not easy for most people to confess

Christ during persecutions. Remember the Parable of the Sower that talks about people who accepted Christ speedily, but when persecution and tribulation came because of the Word of God, and the cares of this world and the deceitfulness of riches overtook them, they denied Christ (Matt. 13:1-23; 1 Tim. 6:6-12). Most people will be in position to be baptized, and sick people who are able to be baptized in Christ's name after being baptized in the name of the Father and of the Son and of the Holy Ghost should not refuse to be baptized over again in Christ's name. Why wouldn't a person make sure that they are baptized correctly before they die due to illness? Often in life, when doing something will help but not hurt or hinder, then we should certainly do it (Acts 2:36-39; 8:14-17; 10:42-48; 19:1-6; John 3:3-7).

God will forgive some people even if they are not baptized properly or not baptized at all, because the Lord has mercy on whom he will and he hardens whom he will (Rom. 9:14-21; Prov. 21:1; John 9:39 - 41). When God hardens the heart of some people instead of having mercy on them, that means that they have sinned so wickedly that God is sending them to hell, and that he is not allowing them to turn to him with a mind to live holy. And God knows that most evil-hearted people will not turn to him wholeheartedly anyway. But most of us must be signed, sealed, and about to be delivered. In other words, our names must be signed in the Book of Life, the book must be sealed, and we must be on your way to heaven, daily (John 6:26-27; 1 Cor. 9:2; 2 Cor. 1:21-22; Eph. 1:13; 4:30; 2 Tim. 2:19).

We must be confirmed, preserved, and blameless (1 Cor. 1:8; 1 Thess. 5:23). Your name must not only be on the church roll, but in the Book of Life (Isa. 44:5). If you put money in a savings account, that money is being saved. If you put money on a bench at the bus stop, it will most likely be lost. Someone may give the money back to you because that happens sometimes, but not often. The same applies to people who are not saved by being signed, sealed, and delivered in the Book of Life (Rev. 20:12-15; Heb. 12:23; Mal. 3:16).

The grace of God that brings salvation has appeared to all people (Titus 2:11–15). Do not receive the grace of God in vain, because our God is a consuming fire and a jealous God (2 Cor. 6:1–10; Heb. 12:28–29; Jude 1:4; Deut. 4:24).

Grace, which is undeserving love and blessings, has been benefited by every human being and grace will save some people who did not serve the Lord their whole life, because first shall be last and last shall be first (Matt. 19:29–30; 20:15–16; Luke 2:34; 13:23–30; Ps. 75:6–7).

It is everyone's decision to take advantage of God's grace. Do not think that anyone is saved because God has healed them or delivered them from trouble. Jesus healed people all the time in the Bible, but that did not mean that they were saved. Jesus told them after he healed them, "Sin no more, or a worse thing will happen to you" (John 5:1–14; 8:3–12; Matt. 11:20–24; 12:43–45).

But some people immediately followed Jesus after he healed them (Matt. 20:34; Mark 10:52). We must be strong in the grace of God, not weak, and not use grace as an excuse to sin (2 Tim. 2:1).

WE ARE BORN IN SIN, BUT AREN'T BABIES BORN INNOCENT?

Jesus says he shed his blood for the remission of sins (Matt. 26:28; Acts 2:38). And because Christ died for our sins, we must repent for the remission of sins (Acts 2:36–39; 8:14–17; 10:42–48; 19:1–6; John 3:3–7).

This means that your willful sin, sins from mistakes and errors, sins committed unaware, and the sins that you inherited from Adam are forgiven after you are baptized in the name of Christ. It has been said that we are born into sin. How can this be when we have done no good or bad in the womb, or as newborn babies (Rom. 9:11). The Bible says that God made everyone righteous, but mankind has made so many wicked inventions that influence people to sin (Eccles. 7:26–29; Ps. 33:13–15).

We are born into Adam's sins. If you do not get baptized in the name of Christ, you still have Adam's sins, no matter how you repent for your own sins. By Adam's disobedience, everyone became guilty of sin, because Adam ate of the tree of knowledge causing all of us to know that we did something wrong when we sin, and our knowledge of sin causes us to die like Adam and Eve died. But by the obedience of Jesus, everyone has the chance to live a righteous life and to live forever (Rom. 5:12–21; 1 Cor. 15:20–21). Christ died and rose from the dead for you! When you repent, you repent for your sins, and when you get baptized in the name of Jesus, the Lord washes away the sins of Adam and your own sins. At that point, you are a new creature—you are born again. The old you and Adam's sins are dead, and all things are new (Rom. 6; 1 Pet. 1:23; 1 John 2:29; 5:4, 18). People who commit sin are of the devil, just as Eve obeyed the devil when she convinced Adam to eat of the tree of knowledge (1 John 3:8–10). Sin is of the devil and not of God (1 John 3:8–10; John 8:34–47; 1 Tim. 5:15). They who are born of flesh is flesh, like Adam, and they who are born again of the water and of the Spirit are spirit, like Christ (John 3:1–6; Rom. 8:5–14). Christ died for all people, so they who live should not live unto themselves, but unto Christ who died for them and rose again (1 John 2:2–4; Acts 17:26; Heb. 2:9; Rom. 5:6–9; 8:32; Isa. 53; John 11:47–57; 2 Cor. 5:15; Acts 10).

We must live a holy and sanctified life separated from the things of the world (John 17:14–19; 15:18–19). "An unjust person is an abomination to the righteous, and the righteous is an abomination to the wicked" (Prov. 29:27). True religion is to go unspotted from the world (James 1:26–27; Isa. 1:15 – 20). "Let us cleanse ourselves from all filthiness of the flesh and spirit, perfecting holiness in the fear of God" (2 Cor. 7:1). Without holiness, no human can see God (Heb. 12:14–15; Rom. 12:1–2; 2 Tim. 2:15).

A friend of the world is God's enemy (James 4:4; John 15:18, 19; 1 John 3:13; Rom. 6; 8:1–16; Gal. 5:16–26; 1 Pet. 2:11; 1 Cor. 1:10; 2:9–16; Rom. 15:5–6).

CHILDREN AND BAPTISM

Concerning children, Jesus says that we should not forbid children to be baptized (Matt. 19:13-14). If kids are to be baptized, they must be immersed in water like Jesus and everyone else in the Bible (Acts 2:36-39; 8:14-17; 10:42-48; 19:1-6; John 3:3-7).

Sprinkling and pouring is not a proper baptism, and it was never done in the Bible. Kids must be old enough to understand that they must strive to not commit willful sin anymore (Mic. 2:1; Ps. 19:12-14; Rom. 1:18-32; 2 Thess. 2:10-15).

We are all saved by grace, but Rom. 6:1-6 tells us that grace shall not always continue and that we should remain new creatures after we are baptized into Christ. Parents and pastors often baptize children too young, and they later go out and sin again willfully, and the Bible tells us that there remains no more sacrifice for sin when we sin willfully after learning the truth (Heb. 10:26-29). Jesus says that if a person starts to build a building, they must finish it, or other people will mock and laugh (Luke 14:26-30). The same applies to us when we are baptized. We must finish what we started, in holiness and sanctification. The Bible says that it is best not to get baptized in the first place if we do not plan to live free of habitual and willful sin (Heb. 10:26; 2 Pet. 2:19-22; Rom. 1:18-32; 2 Thess. 2:10-15).

Those same scriptures tell us that when people are baptized and later backslide, they will end up in worse shape than before. The Bible tells us to sin no more or a worse thing will happen to us (John 5:14; 8:3-11; James 5:13-20; 2 Pet. 2:20; Isa. 57:11-12).

So, we need to be careful about baptizing children before they understand what they are doing. It is okay to have them blessed or christened, as Jesus was when he was an infant, but notice that Christ did not get baptized during his christening (Luke 2:25-39). Jesus was not baptized until he was thirty years old (Luke 3:21-23). If a child is christened, it is about equal to being blessed, and the child will still need to be baptized in the future, as Jesus was. If children are truly ready to be baptized, do not forbid them (Matt. 19:14). Not only does this save their souls, but also it prevents them from being natural bastards if they were born out of wedlock, and spiritual bastards if they were born in wedlock to unsaved parents. Even kids who were born in wedlock to unsaved parents are spiritual bastards, until they and/or their parents get baptized properly (1 Cor. 7:14; 2 Cor. 6:14-18; Heb. 12:8).

Before Christ died for our sins, a bastard was not allowed to enter the congregation of the Lord (Deut. 23:2). Kids are often baptized without understanding and without true repentance. They often sin willfully later in life and live in sin for years. Jesus says this is like a dog returning to eat its own vomit (2 Pet. 2:20-22). Kids who do not know the difference between good and evil will go to heaven anyway if they should die (Deut. 1:35-39; Matt. 19:13-14). Even in the Old Testament, only people with understanding were held responsible for what the preacher was saying (Neh. 8:1-3). And all the children and teenagers were allowed to go into the promised land when their parents were not allowed (Num. 32:11-12). There is no such thing as kids needing to be baptized to wash away sins that they inherited from their parents (Exod. 32:30-35; Ezek. 14:12-20; 18:14-32).

Kids should not be baptized to take the place of the circumcision, because circumcision is spiritually no longer needed (Col. 2:11; 1 Cor. 7:19).

CHRIST IS HOLY AND SANCTIFIED LIKE WE SHOULD BE

Christ commands that we live in true holiness and righteousness "all the days of our life" (Luke 1:74–75; Eph. 4:21–32).

It is written, "Be ye holy, for I am holy" (1 Pet. 1:14–16; 1 Tim. 2:8; Eph. 5:25 – 27; Rev. 20:6).

Righteous God loves righteousness (Ps. 11:7). The Holy Scripture says, "Let no one deceive you, they who live righteously are righteous, for God is righteous, and they who sin are of the devil" (1 John 3:5–10). God is righteous, and everyone who strives to live right is born again (1 John 2:29; 3:7). God gives the Holy Spirit to people who obey him (Acts 5:32; Luke 11:13; John 1:1, 14; 14:13–18, 26–27; Col. 3:16; 1 John 2:5, 7, 14).

We must get rid of anger, wrath, malice, blasphemy, and filthy words (Col. 3:8). God says, "I the Lord speak righteousness, I declare things that are right" (Isa. 45:19; Ps. 19:8). The Bible says that we must be holy in all manner of conversation (1 Pet. 1:15; 1 Cor. 15:33; 2 Pet. 3:10–12; Ps. 19:12–14; Prov. 8:5–8; 1 Cor. 15:33; Eph. 4:21–32; Isa. 33:15–16; Mal. 2:5–6).

PEOPLE WHO DO NOT OBEY THE APOSTLES' DOCTRINE ARE SPIRITUALLY BLIND

The Bible says that if the apostles' doctrine is hidden, it is hidden from people who are lost (2 Cor. 4:3–5). God has hidden this from some wise and prudent people but revealed it to many babes and common people (Matt. 11:25; Luke 19:37–42; 1 Cor. 1:26–32).

If you do not obey God's Word, he will blind you, or allow the devil to blind you, and cause you to not understand it (John 12:40; 2 Cor. 4:4; Eph. 4:18).

Blessed are you whom God has caused to understand (Matt. 13:10–17). The Bible says in all your getting, get understanding (Prov. 4:7; Jer. 9:23–24). May the Lord Jesus Christ continue to bless all people who are not baptized in Christ's name, and who reject the baptism in Christ's name and his solid foundation, strong cornerstone, and pillar (Isa. 28:16; Ps. 118:17–24; Matt. 21:42; Acts 4:10–11; 1 Pet. 2:6–7).

WHY DOES GOD WORK IN THREE REVELATIONS & MANIFESTATIONS OF HIMSELF?

Why did God choose to operate as one Spirit with three different revelations of himself? It is brilliant of Father God to operate this way. God the Son sets examples for us with no excuses. The invisible things of God from the creation of the world are clearly seen, being understood by the things that are made, even his eternal power and "Godhead" so that people are without excuse (Rom. 1:18–32; Col. 2:9; Acts 17:24–31).

God the Son was preordained before the foundation of the world but manifested in these last days for our sake (1 Pet. 1:20). Father God operates as God the Holy Ghost so he can be our Comforter, in the name of Christ, and a protector and strengthener who remains on earth with us to our benefit (John 14:16–26; 15:26–27; 16:7–16; Acts 9:31; Ps. 94:19; 2 Thess. 2:16–17).

The revelation of God the Father, God the Son, and God the Holy Ghost also allows God to be in heaven, on earth, and throughout the entire universe, including all galaxies, planets, stars, and moons at the same time (1 Pet. 3:18–20; 2 Pet. 2:4–9; Ps. 8; Matt. 10:32–33; 12:50; 16:17; 18:10, 14; 23:9).

God the Father sent God the Son in the form of flesh and blood to be an example to us on how to serve only one God who is God Almighty and to serve him without honoring idols because idolaters will not inherit the kingdom of God (Eph. 5:5; 1 Cor. 6:9; Rev. 21:8, 27; 22:14–15; Gal. 5:19–21; 1 Sam. 15:23; Col.3:1–6).

God the Son is also our confirmation, proof, and validation of the resurrection of the dead of not only Christ but of all dead people when Christ returns (Acts 24:15; Dan.12:1–3; Matt. 13:47–50; 25:31–46; John 5:24–29; Rev. 22:10–13; 1 Cor. 15:20–28).

God the Father also reveals himself as God the Son to illustrate to his creation how we should live and how we should honor our parents and to be obedient to godly parents (Eph. 6:1–4; Col. 3:18–20; Exod. 20:12) and how good children can someday inherit the possessions and power of their parents to work hard in life to achieve their goals and to do well with their inheritance (Prov. 13:22; John 16:15; Luke 15:11–32).

God the Son also teaches married couples how to love, honor, support, and respect each other as husband and wife, being one flesh, just as the Father, Son, and Holy Ghost are one Spirit. Christ also illustrates to us how the church, the family, and certain organizations can consist of many members, but we should still operate as one (Rev. 19:7; 21:2, 9; 22:17; 2 Cor. 11:2–3; Eph. 4:4–6; 5:23, 27; Isa. 54:4–10; Jer. 3:6–15, 22; 31:27–37; Hosea 1:2; Ps. 73:27–28).

God the Son is also an example of how to resist temptation, to be humble, to forgive, to be compassionate, how to be tolerant of other people, how to be merciful, to give, to help people, and to love one another, including our enemies. God the Son showed us how to resist temptation when the devil offered Christ fame, riches, power, and earthly kingdoms, but Christ used Bible scriptures to rebuke the devil, and so should we (Luke 4:1–21). The life of God the Son teaches us how to handle adversity, affliction, false accusations, poverty, homelessness, persecution for living godly, to not oppress people, and how to deal with being an oppressed person like Christ was oppressed (2 Cor. 8:9; Phil. 4:19; Lev. 12:6–8; Luke 2:21–24; 9:58; 21:36–37; 22:39–46; Matt. 25:31–46; Isa. 53).

Christ also teaches us how to handle not being physically attractive, and the Bible tells us that Christ was not physically attractive nor was he handsome (Isa. 52:13–15, 53; Heb. 2:16–18; 4:15; 1 Pet. 2:22).

God the Son chose not to visit the earth as a handsome man because people would have favored him for good looks and not because he is the Son of God. And he did not visit the earth as a middle – class person, a rich person, or a powerful politician because people would have favored him for those reasons. Job was more one of the most righteous people to ever live, and he was wealthy, but his example of a sanctified life was not as strong as God visiting the earth as the Son of God; neither was Job's sacrifice nor suffering as great. God the Father knew that people who seek him will respect God the Son, and they live more righteously because of God the Son's examples than the examples of Job and other righteous people in the Bible.

CHRIST & GOD ARE ONE, SO WHAT HAPPENED TO CHRIST'S HUMAN BODY AFTER HE WENT TO HEAVEN?

Another question that some people may ask regarding Father God operating as one Spirit with three different revelations of himself is, "If God and Christ are the same, what happened to the human body of Christ?" When Christ died, rose from the dead, and went back to heaven, the same thing probably happened to his body that happens to our body when we die; it is dissolved, and we become absent from the body but present with God (2 Pet. 1:12–15; 3:10–18; 2 Cor. 5:1–10).

Our "spirit" goes back to God who gave it, just as God the Son's "Spirit" returned to heaven from whence he came (Gen. 2:7; 7:22; Eccles. 12:7; Job 27:1–6; 34:14–15; Dan. 5:23).

The human body of Christ did have a human side, or a human element, and it was characterized when God the Father sometimes refers to Christ as the Son of David and the Son of Man. This is done because Christ was the son of Mary and the adopted son of Joseph and because he was a descendent of David, according to the flesh, according to his human side. Christ declared to be the Son of God with power, according to the "Spirit" of holiness (Matt. 9:6, 27; 15:22; 16:13; Rom. 1:3–4; Dan. 7:13–15).

There is one mediator between God and mankind, the man Jesus Christ, but the man Jesus Christ operated with the Holy Spirit of the one God Almighty inside of him (1 Tim. 2:5; 1 John 2:1; 5:7; Gen. 17:1).

Another characterization of the human side of Christ happened before he was arrested and on the cross when Christ asked Father God to remove his pain, suffering, and eventual death. At that moment, he suffered from anxiety to the point that sweat fell from his body like drops of blood, but the human side of Christ was obedient to Father God and said to God the Father, "Not my will, but your will be done" (Matt. 26:36–42; Luke 22:39–46).

God the Son would not have been worried about what humans would do to him when they arrested him because he is God. That was the human side of Christ suffering from anxiety. He later said to God the Father while on the cross, "Into your hands, I commit my 'spirit'" (Luke 23:44–46). Then he took his last breath and died. In this instance, "spirit" is spelled with a lowercase "s." When the word "Spirit" is spelled with an uppercase "S," the term always refers to only God the Father, God the Son, and God the Holy Spirit. When spelled with a lowercase "s," the term "spirit" refers to our spirit that is inside of our bodies and to all other spirits. Therefore, the human body of Christ was a vessel and temple for God the Son to dwell in, and when the human body of Christ died, his "sprit" returned to God who gave it. And while the dead human body of Christ was in the grave, the "Spirit" of God the Son visited a God made prison for "spirits" and preached to the "spirits" who disobeyed God when Noah preached to them before God destroyed the earth by water (1 Pet. 3:18–20; 2 Pet. 2:4–9).

Angels who went against God are also in a dark God made prison and in chains made for spirits (Jude 1:5–6; Rev. 9:11; 12:7–12; Luke 10:17–20; Col. 2:18; Rom. 8:38–39; Matt. 9:34;

12:24; 25:41; 1 Pet. 3:18–20; 2 Pet. 2:4).

God hid the dead body of Moses, seemingly because some people would idolize Moses's body just as some people preserve and idolize the bodies of certain other people who lived when the Bible was written. Even though God hid the body of Moses, the "spirit" of Moses appeared to Christ on earth and talked with Christ (Matt. 17:1–13). Also, when the "spirit" of Moses met with Christ, the "spirit" of Elijah was also in the meeting. Elijah's body was taken to heaven by God in a whirlwind hundreds of years before Christ ministered on earth, and Elijah's body was not found either even though a group of fifty men searched for him throughout the mountains for three days (2 Kings 2:1–18). Melchizedek had no mother or father, but he appeared on earth and disappeared from earth according to the will of God, and there was never a baby Melchizedek nor a dead body after his departure (Heb. 7:1–3). But there was a baby Jesus, although there is not a dead body of Jesus after Christ went back to heaven. Christ did not glorify himself to become High Priest, but God said to him, "You are my Son. Today I have begotten you." God also says in another place, "You are a priest forever after the order of Melchizedek," who in the days of Christ's flesh, when he had offered up prayers and supplications with strong crying and tears to God, who was able to save him from death and was heard because of his godly fear, though he was a Son, yet he learned obedience by the things that he suffered. And having been made perfect, he became the author of eternal salvation to all who obey him, called of God a High Priest, "after the order of Melchizedek" (Heb. 5:5–10). God, who at certain times and in different places, spoke in the past to humans by the prophets, but in these last days, God speaks to us by his Son, through whom he made the worlds. Having become so much more than the angels as he has, by inheritance, obtained a more excellent name than them. To which of the angels did God ever say, "You are my Son, today I have begotten you?" (Heb. 1:1–2, 4–13). God did not put the world to come in subjection to angels. But one testified in a certain place, saying, "What is man that God is mindful of him, or the son of man that God visits him? God made him a little lower than the angels. God crowned him with glory and honor and set him over the works of his hands. God has put all things in subjection under his feet." In that, he put all in subjection under him; he left nothing that is not put under him. But now, we see not yet all things under him. But we see Jesus, who was made a little lower than the angels for the suffering of death, crowned with glory and honor, that he, by the grace of God, should taste death for every human (Heb. 2:5–10). It does not matter what happened to the human body of Christ after God the Son went back to heaven to rule the entire universe just as it does not matter what happened to the bodies of Moses, Melchizedek, and Elijah. God uses people as holy vessels and temples that will be dissolved and go back to the dust after death. All that matters is that Christ rose from the dead, and that when we rise from the dead, our soul and "spirit" goes to heaven, where our one God of the Father, Son, and Holy Ghost is on the throne, and these three are one (1 John 5:7–8). The Bible says that Christ returned to heaven and sat on the throne of God and on the right-hand side of God the Father (Rom. 8:34; Col. 3:1–2; Heb. 1:3, 13; 8:1; 10:12; 12:2; 1 Pet. 3:22).

But in the book of Revelation, John saw only One on the throne (Rev. 4:2). John also said that the One who he saw was the Son of God, and that Christ told him, "I am the First and the Last, who was dead but is now alive forevermore. Amen. I have the keys of hell and death (Rev. 1:11–19; 22:13). How can Father God be the first and the last and besides the Father there is no God if Christ is also the first and the last and is called God (Isa. 41:4; 44:6; 48:12; Heb.1:8)? The answer is that they are the same Spirit, and God reveals himself in our day and age as God the Son and as God the Holy Ghost and with the same name (Zech. 14:9; John 5:43; 10:25; 14:26; 1 John 2:23). As stated earlier, all power is in the hands of God the Son who now visits the earth to call people to holiness and to chastise, to destroy, and to punish (1 Cor. 15:24–28; Phil. 2:5–11; Ps. 8; Heb. 2:5–9; 4:12; Matt. 28:18; Rev. 1:16; 2:12–16; 19:15, 21; Eph. 1:20–23; 6:10–20; Col. 2:10;

John 16:15).

God the Holy Ghost is with us always, even until the end of the world, and is our Comforter, guidance, power, protection, and strength, in the name of Christ (Matt. 28:19–20). It has been erroneously said that the original apostles baptized people in the name of the Lord Jesus Christ during the first ever baptism to start the first ever church congregation to try to get the ancient Jews to accept Christ (Acts 2:36–47). That is not true. About three thousand people were baptized in Christ's name on that one day, and additional people were baptized daily. Peter told them that the baptism in Christ's name and the gift of the Holy Ghost is for the ancient Jews, their children, and to everyone, even people in faraway nations (Acts 2:36–47; 8:14–17; 10:47–48; 19:1–10; John 3:3–7).

Also, the Apostle Paul baptized Gentiles in the name of the Lord Jesus Christ even though he had never met Peter nor any of Christ's original apostles. Paul did not meet Peter until three years after he started baptizing Gentiles in the name of Christ. Therefore, Paul was not taught by any human to baptize people in Christ's name, but Christ himself taught Paul to baptize people in the name of the Lord Jesus Christ (Gal. 1:11–24; 2:1, 7–10; Acts 19:1–10; John 3:3–7).

Therefore, the baptism in Christ's name was not performed only to convince the ancient Jews to accept Christ. But it may be that Christ revealed himself standing on the right hand of the glory of God to convince certain ancient Jews of Christ's resurrection when Stephen being full of the Holy Ghost saw Jesus the Son of man in the sky (Acts 7:51–60). Obviously, Stephen did not see God because no one has seen God and lived. Secondly, Stephen only saw the glory of God, and he did not see a throne like John saw when John saw One on the throne (Rev. 4:2). Thirdly, Stephen saw a revelation of Christ standing at the right hand of God, which could mean the right hand of power, like in other scriptures that say, "Christ, the power of God, and the wisdom of God," and that Christ sat on the right side of the Majesty, and Majesty means royal power (Heb. 1:1–3; 8:1; 12:2; 1

Cor. 1:22–24; Col. 3:1–2; Eph. 1:19–23; Ps. 8:9).

The Prophet Micah also spoke of God the Son having the power of the majesty of the Lord. Micah said hundreds of years before Christ walked the earth, "But you, Bethlehem, though you are small, yet out of you shall come the one to be ruler in Israel, whose goings forth are from of old, from everlasting. He shall stand and feed his flock in the strength of the Lord, in the majesty of the name of the Lord His God. And they shall abide. For He shall be great to the ends of the earth" (Mic. 5:2–4). God the Son now has all power in his own hand, so there is no need for him to physically or literally sat on the right side of God the Father on the throne. God the Son went to heaven and sat on the right hand of the power of God the Father, meaning omnipotent power being one God, just as John saw God the Son on the throne as one God (Rev. 1:11–19; 4:2). Jesus says, "You will see the Son of man sitting at the right hand of the Power and coming on the clouds of heaven" (Matt. 24:27–44; 26:64). Christ says that if anyone is ashamed to stand for his Word, he will be ashamed of them when Christ, the Son of man, comes in the glory of his Father with the holy angels (Mark 8:38). Therefore, when Stephen saw the Son of man standing on the right hand of the glory of God, he saw Jesus, the Son of man, standing on the right hand of the Power of God and of the glory of God (Matt. 26:64; Mark 8:38; Acts 7:51–60).

"LET US MAKE MAN IN OUR OWN IMAGE," WAS SPOKEN TO WHO?

When God said in Genesis 1:26, "Let us make man in our own image," who was he talking too? Bible scholars from several denominations have opinions. Some people believe that God was talking to himself. Some people believe that God was talking to himself with God the Son in his distant future plans because he knew that he would send Christ as a sacrifice for the people who he created and love. Other people say that he was talking to angels. And some people say that he was speaking directly to his Son, Christ. It is amazing how many Christians from different denominations agree that God was talking to himself or to God the Son as part of the one Godhead (Rom. 1:18–32; Col. 2:9; Acts 17:24–31).

Many of those same people do not baptize in Christ's name, and they try to acknowledge a trinity that they admit is not in the Bible. The answer to the question is that God the Father was talking to God the Son and to himself because they are the same one Spirit and have the same one name in our generations (Zech. 14:9; Eph. 4:4–6; John 5:43; 10:25; 14:26; 1 John 2:23; 5:7–8).

The earth, all other planets, and the entire universe was made by God the Father through Jesus Christ (John 1:10; Heb. 1:2; 11:3; 1 Pet. 1:20).

There is only one God, of whom are all things, and one Lord

Jesus Christ, through whom are all things (1 Cor. 8:6). As stated earlier, God the Son was preordained before the foundation of the world but manifested in these last days for our sake (1 Pet. 1:20). God says, "Beside me there is no God and no Savior, and before me there was no God formed, and neither shall there be after me (Isa. 43:10–11; 44:6; Deut. 6:4; James 2:19; Jude 1:25; Mark 12:29; John 10:30).

Christ also says that he is the beginning and the ending, the first and the last (Rev. 1:8, 11; 21:6; 22:13). Therefore, God and Christ are obviously one. Christ is the mediator between Father God and humans (1 Tim. 2:5). The Bible says that a mediator cannot be a mediator of one, but that God is still one (Gal. 3:20; 1 Cor. 8:6; Acts 4:12). To clarify, it is impossible for a mediator to be the middle – person between God and humans because the mediator is God himself. God the Son and God the Holy Ghost are revelations of God the Father, but the same one Spirit and the same one name (Eph. 4:4–6; Zech. 14:9; John 5:43; 10:25; 14:26; 1 John 2:23; 5:7–8).

David said by the Holy Ghost, "My Lord said to my Lord, 'Sit on my right side until I make your enemies my footstool'" (Mark 12:36; Acts 2:34–35). Again, God the Father was speaking to God the Son, or to himself, which is the same. And just as the capitalized word "Spirit" refers to only God the Father, God the Son, and God the Holy Spirit, the capitalized word "Lord" also refers only to God. Every knee shall bow, and every tongue shall confess that Jesus Christ is Lord, to the glory of God the Father (Phil. 2:5–11). At another time, when God talked to Christ, Father God told Christ that the Son is God (Heb. 1:8). God told Christ, "Your throne, O God, is forever and ever" (Heb.1:8). Once again, God is talking to himself as God and to God the Son as the same one God (Gen. 1:26; John 1:10; Heb. 1:2; 11:3). And when Christ says that people who overcome shall sit with him on his throne just as he sat with his Father on the Father's throne, that scripture mirrors and reflects another scripture that says, "No one comes to God the Father without going through God the Son" (Rev. 3:21; John 14:6). How can we sit on a separate throne with the Son of God after God the Son delivers the kingdom of heaven into the hands of God the Father and after all power goes back from God the Son to God the Father when the earth is destroyed? In other words, even if the Father and the Son were two different Spirits, Christ would not be on a throne in heaven because all power goes back into the hands of the God the Father when the earth is destroyed. All things including God the Son will be subject to God the Father, and the Father will be all in all, (1 Cor. 15:24–28). There is one body and one Spirit, one Lord, one faith, one baptism, one God and Father of all, who is above all and through all and in you all (Eph. 4:4–6).

God the Father gave God the Son a name above every name, and that is because they have the same name, which is Jesus Christ (Zech. 14:9; Phil. 2:5–11; John 5:43; 10:25; 14:26; 1 John 2:23; 5:7–8).

It is impossible for God the Son to have a name that is above God the Father. The prophet Zechariah prophesized of the coming of Christ when he said, "The Lord shall be King over all the earth. In that day it shall be—the Lord is one, and his name one" (Zech. 12:10; 14:9; John 19:31–37; Rev. 1:4–8).

God the Son now has all power and authority, and that does not mean that God the Father is weak, sick, dead, lazy, or have taken a back seat to what goes on in heaven, earth, hell, and the entire universe, but it is impossible for Christ to have all power, and Father God still be omnipotent, omnipresent, and omniscient without them being the same one Spirit (Col. 2:10; 1 Cor. 15:24–28; Phil. 2:5–11; Eph. 1:20–23; 4:4–6; 6:10–20; Matt. 28:18; Heb. 2:5–9; 4:12; Rev. 1:16; 2:12–16; 19:15, 21).

God Almighty is mysterious, and he would not be Almighty God if he was not mysterious. The Bible says, "Without controversy, great is the mystery of godliness." The Bible says that God's ways are past finding out, and that his ways and thoughts are much higher than ours (Rom. 11:33; Isa. 55:8). God was manifest in the flesh, justified in the Spirit, seen of angels, preached to the Gentiles, believed on in the world, and received up into glory (1 Tim. 3:16). The Apostle Paul also wrote, "To him who is of power to establish you according to my gospel, and the preaching of Jesus Christ, according to the revelation of the mystery, which was kept secret since the world began, but now made manifest, according to the commandment of the everlasting God, made known to all nations for obedience of the faith—to the only wise God be glory through Jesus Christ forever. Amen" (Rom. 16:25-27). God is mysterious in many ways, but it is safe to say that the revelation of the Father, Son, and Holy Ghost was one of the mysteries kept secret since the world began because although the worlds were made through God the Son, God the Son was not manifested for thousands of years (1 Pet. 1:20; John 1:10; Heb. 1:2; 11:3; Col. 1:15).

But the first and second coming of God the Son was and is prophesized (Isa. 7:14; 9:6-7; 52:13-5, 53; Dan. 7:9, 13, 22; 9:24-27; 12:1-4; Gen. 49:9-10; Num. 24:17; Zech. 14:9; 1 Thess. 4:13-18; 1 Cor. 15:50-58).

The Apostle Peter said that some of the Apostle Paul's writings are hard to be understood, but that they are valid and righteous, that Christ shall return for people who are without spot and blameless, and that some people struggle with the apostles' doctrine to their own destruction (2 Pet. 3:14-16). God the Father made the world and all planets by God the Son (John 1:10; Heb. 1:2, 8-13; 11:3; 1 Pet. 1:20).

The Son is the image of the invisible God, the firstborn over all creation (Col. 1:15). Paul also said, "We speak the wisdom of God in a mystery, even the hidden wisdom, which God ordained before the world unto our glory, which none of the princes of this world knew. If they had known it, they would not have crucified the Lord of glory. But God has revealed them to us through his Spirit. For the Spirit searches all things, yes, the deep things of God. These things we also speak, not in words, which man's wisdom teaches, but which the Holy Spirit teaches, comparing spiritual things with spiritual. But the natural person does not receive the things of the Spirit of God because they are foolishness to them, nor can they know them, because spiritual things are spiritually discerned. Who has known the mind of the Lord that they may instruct him? But we have the mind of Christ (1 Cor. 1:22–24; 2:6–10; Luke 23:34).

The Apostle Paul wrote, "I was made a minister, according to the gift of the grace of God given to me by the effectual working of his power. That I should preach to the Gentiles the unsearchable riches of Christ, and to make all people see what is the fellowship of the mystery which from the beginning of the world has been hid in God, who created all things by Jesus Christ, to the intent that now the principalities and powers in heavenly places might be known by the church the manifold wisdom of God, according to the eternal purpose which he purposed in Christ Jesus our Lord" (Eph. 3:7–12). Furthermore, the Apostle Paul wrote, "I became a minister according to the stewardship from God, which was given to me for you, to fulfill the Word of God, the mystery which has been hidden from ages and from generations, but now has been revealed to his saints" (Col. 1:25–26). Paul also said that we wanted people to have a full assurance of understanding, to the knowledge of the mystery of God, both of the Father, and of Christ, in whom are hidden all the treasures of wisdom and knowledge (Col. 2:2–3).

WHAT IS THE NAME OF THE FATHER, SON, AND HOLY SPIRIT?

God went by a few names in the Old Testament, including God Almighty and Almighty God (Gen. 17:1; 35:11). The name God Almighty is not used in the New Testament of the Authorized King James Version of the Bible other than in the book of Revelation (Rev. 1:8; 4:8; 11:17; 15:3; 16:7, 14; 19:15; 21:22).

Therefore, the name God Almighty was used first in the book of Genesis, which is the first book of the Bible, and the book of Revelation, which is the last book of the Bible. The closest reference to the name God Almighty outside of the book of Revelation in the New Testament is one time when the Apostle Paul quoted God's words and referred to him as Lord Almighty (2 Cor. 6:17–18). Maybe Christ and the apostles never used the name God Almighty in the gospels because they knew that ministers would baptize people in the name of God Almighty instead of in the name of the Lord Jesus Christ (Acts 2:36–42; 8:14–17; 10:47–48; 19:2–5; John 3:3–7).

Jehovah is another name of God from the Old Testament and is written in only a few scriptures (Exod. 6:3; Ps. 83:18; Isa. 12:2; 26:4). Some versions of the Bible use the term Lord instead of Jehovah. The term Yahweh is used instead of Jehovah in some versions of the Bible and is often used in the Hebrew Bible. Hebrew letters have only consonants but no vowels, and over time, vowels were inserted to create the words Yahweh and

Jehovah from JHVH and JHWH, thus also replacing the letter "Y" with "J" and creating the word Yahweh from YHWH and YHVH. Jehovah-jireh, Jehovah-nissi, Jehovah-shalom, and Jehovah-shammah are not names of God (Gen. 22:14; Exod. 17:11, 15; Judg. 6:24; Ezek. 48:35).

It should be noted that God's original chosen people the ancient Hebrews and ancient Israelites were blinded from the Christian Faith in part so God can call the entire world to repentance (Rom. 11:25–36; Isa. 55:8). If God had allowed ancient Hebrews, ancient Israelites, and ancient Jews to accept Christ, they would have stood against allowing other people to become Christians. Because for thousands of years, God taught ancient Hebrews, ancient Jews, and ancient Israelites to be separate from the rest of the world (Acts 10). There are other names of God in the Hebrew Bible, but God does not go by any of those names anymore. In our generations, God goes by the name Jesus Christ (John 5:43; 10:25, 30; 14:26; 1 John 2:23; 5:7–8).

Even in the Old Testament and in the Hebrew Bible, it was prophesized that "the Lord shall be King over all the earth. In that day it shall be—the Lord is one, and his name one." And that God shall be pierced while hanging on the cross (Zech. 12:10; 14:9; John 19:31–37).

Those prophesies were fulfilled when God the Son was pierced on the cross as King of the entire universe, (John 16:15; 19:28–37; Rev. 1:4–8; Col. 2:10; 1 Cor. 15:24–28; Phil. 2:5–11; Eph. 1:20–23; 4:4–6; Matt. 28:18; Heb. 2:5–9).

The name Immanuel had several purposes. One purpose was to indicate to the world that God is with us, just as Christ says that he is with us always, even to the end of the world (Isa. 7:14; 8:8; Matt. 1:18–25; 28:19–20). Also, the name Immanuel was given to conceal Jesus from people who would crown him too soon and from others who would crucify him too soon (John 7:1–9; Matt. 8:4; 16:20; 17:9; Mark 7:36; 8:30; Luke 8:56).

Also, to prevent the baby Jesus from being killed by an evil king who killed all the male children two years of age and younger to try to prevent the child Jesus from growing up (Matt.

2:13–16; Rev. 12:1–8; Exod. 1:15–22; 2:1–10).

An angel told Joseph that the child's name is Immanuel to fulfill prophesy, but that same angel told Joseph to name the child Jesus, which was a popular name in those days, and it prevented the world from knowing that the child was really Immanuel (Matt. 1:18–25). There was a disciple of the Apostle Paul who was named Jesus, but they called in Justus instead of Jesus in honor of the Lord (Col. 4:11). Therefore, we baptize in the name of the Lord Jesus Christ because he is Lord of all (Dan. 9:25–26; John 1:41; 4:25).

Another name that God went by in the Old Testament was "I Am" (Exod. 3:13–15). Christ also says that he himself is "I Am" (John 8:58). That is because they are the same Spirit with the same name in the New Testament and throughout all generations after the New Testament was written. Father God, and God the Son is "I Am" because he is omnipotent, omniscient, omnipresent, one God, one Spirit, with one name (Eph. 4:4–6). When Moses asked God what his name is, God told Moses, "I Am That I Am." God went on to say that this is his name forever, and this is my memorial unto all generations (Exod. 3:13–15). Generations after God the Father said that God the Son is now "I Am." God the Son says, "I am with you always, even to the end of the world" (Matt. 28:20). "I am he, the Messiah, the Christ" (John 4:19–26). "I am the bread of life" (John 6:35, 48). "I am the bread which came down from heaven" (John 6:41). "I am the living bread" (John 6:51). "I am the light of the world" (John 8:12). "I am from above" (John 8:23). "I am not of this world" (John 8:23). "Before Abraham was, I Am" (John 8:58). "I am the door" (John 10:9). "I am the resurrection" (John 11:25). "I am the way" (John 14:6). "I am the truth" (John 14:6). "I am the life" (John 14:6; 11:25). "I am the true vine" (John 15:1). "I am Alpha and Omega" (Rev. 1:8). "I am he who lives" (Rev. 1:18). "I am alive forevermore" (Rev. 1:18). Father God says, "I am the Lord who heals" (Exod. 15:26). "I, even I, am he, and there is no God with me. I kill and make alive. I wound and I heal. Neither is there any who can deliver out of my hand" (Deut. 32:39). "I, the Lord, the first, and with the last, I am he" (Isa. 41:4). "I am he. Before me there was no God formed, neither shall there be after me" (Isa. 43:10). "I, even I, am the Lord, and beside me there is no savior" (Isa. 43:11). "Before the day was, I am he. And there is none who can deliver out of my hand" (Isa. 43:13). "I am the Lord, and there is no one else. There is no God beside me" (Isa. 45:5). "That they may know from the rising of the sun, and from the west, that there is none beside me. I am the Lord, and there is no one else. I form the light and create darkness. I make peace and create evil. I the Lord do all these things" (Isa. 45:6–7). "Even to your old age, I am he. I will carry you. I have made, and I will bear. Even I will carry and will deliver you" (Isa. 46:3–4). "Remember the former things of old, for I am God, and there is none else. I am God, and there is none like me" (Isa. 46:8–9). "I am for you, and I will turn to you" (Ezek. 36:9). I am the Lord who makes all things (Isa. 44:24). As you can see, the Father, Son, and Holy Spirit have the same name in our generations and have always been the same one Spirit. The rejection of the baptism in the name of the Lord Jesus Christ is deception by the devil who Christ says deceives the whole world because he knows that his time is short (Rev. 12:7–12; Luke 10:18).

Nowadays, Father God comes to us in the name of Jesus Christ (John 5:43; 10:25; 14:26; 1 John 2:23). And God the Holy Ghost, also called the Holy Spirit, always dwells on the earth, and he dwells inside the body of people who obey the Lord (Matt. 28:19–20; Acts 5:32; John 14:13–18, 26–27; Col. 3:16).

Our bodies are temples made for God to dwell in (1 Cor. 3:16–23; 6:9–20). When we are baptized in Christ's name, we become members of the household of God, built on the foundation of the apostles and the prophets, Jesus Christ himself being the chief cornerstone, and the stone that most people reject (Eph. 2:19–22; Ps. 118:22; Matt. 21:42; 1 Pet. 2:7; Acts 4:11–12).

There is one body and one Spirit, one hope, one Lord, one faith, one baptism, one God and Father of all, who is above all, and through all, and in you all who are filled with the Holy Ghost (Eph. 4:4–6). The Father, Son, and Holy Ghost is the great "I Am" because he is all in all, and there is no one else (Isa. 45:5–7; 46:8–9). There is only one God, of whom are all things, and one Lord Jesus Christ, through whom are all things (1 Cor. 8:6; 15:24–28). God said, "Let us make man in our own image, according to our likeness" (Gen. 1:26). But God also says, "Thus says the Lord, your Redeemer, and he who formed you in the womb. I am the Lord, who makes all things, who stretches out the heavens all alone, who spreads abroad the earth by myself" (Isa. 44:24).

CONFESSING WITH YOUR MOUTH, BELIEVING IN YOUR HEART, AND CALLING ON THE NAME OF THE LORD

BELIEVING AND CONFESSING, AND ACCEPTING THE LORD'S SUPPER UNWORTHILY

If all a person must do to be saved is believe, confess, and call on the name of the Lord, why does the Bible say that people become sick and sometimes die when they accept the Lord's Supper while living in sin (1 Cor. 11:23–30)?

WE MUST LIVE HOLY IN THIS PRESENT WORLD

We must also live godly and righteously in this present world (Titus 2:11–12). Remember, the Lord's Prayer says regarding God about us, "Your will be done on earth as it is in heaven" (Matt. 6:10). We must offer the sacrifices of righteousness and put our trust in the Lord while also offering the sacrifices of praise, and to give thanks unto the Lord (Ps. 4:5; Heb. 13:15).

BROKEN PROMISES TO GOD MAKE LIFE WORSE THAN BEFORE

God says it is better to not make promises unto him at all than to make promises and break them, because that could cause more problems in your life, even death (Eccles. 5:2–6; Deut. 23:21–23; Prov. 20:24–25; Jer. 42:1–6, 21–22; 2 Pet. 2:20).

If all we must do to be saved is confess, believe, and call on the Lord, why does the Lord say that we risk dying and going to hell if we do not keep our promises made unto him? "Whatsoever you do, do it wholeheartedly as unto the Lord, and not unto mankind or idols" (Col. 3:17, 23). We must seek glory from God alone, and glory from mankind will eventually come, if it is God's will (John 5:41, 44; 7:18; 12:42–43; 2 Cor. 3:1–4; 1 Thess. 2:4–6).

We must not live by bread or earthly desires and possessions alone, but by every Word of God (Deut. 8:2–3; Luke 4:1–4; John 6:27).

We are not to obey God's Word with partiality (1 Tim. 5:20–21). Jesus says that anyone who obeys his Word shall never die (John 8:51).

We must be doers of the Word and not hearers only (James 1:22–27; Matt. 13:1–23; Acts 17:11–12; Ps. 81:10–16; Jer. 15:15–21; Rev. 10:9–11).

LIVING IN THE FLESH IS WAR AGAINST THE BODY & SOUL

We reap what we sow, in every aspect of life, good or bad (Rom. 2:4–11; Gal. 6:7–10). When we sow to the flesh, we reap trouble to the flesh, but people who sow to the Spirit shall reap everlasting life in heaven (Gal. 6:7–8, 14). Therefore, we must worship God in spirit and in truth and not in the flesh or as a lover of the world (John 4:23–24; Zech. 8:1–8). People who live in the flesh cannot please God (Rom. 8:8). The Spirit is against the flesh and the flesh is against the Spirit (Gal. 5:16–26; 1 Pet. 2:11–12). Flesh and blood cannot inherit the kingdom of heaven, but walking in and living in the Spirit while you are alive allows you to go to heaven (1 Cor. 15:42–52; Gal. 5:16, 24–25; 1 Thess. 4:14–17; John 3:3–7).

When people fail to please God who is in heaven and are lovers of this current world, they are enemies of God (James 4:2–4; John 1:10–12; 15:18–19; 1 John 2:15–17; 3:13).

True religion is to go unspotted from the world (James 1:26–27; Isa. 1:15 – 20). When you become filled with the Holy Spirit inside of your body, greater is Christ in you than they who are in the world (John 16:33; 1 John 4:4). The fruit of the Spirit is goodness, truth, and righteousness and it is a shame to even speak of in a glorifying manner the fleshly sin that sinners do (Eph. 5:9–12). If a sinner does not repent, there shall be no reward for them, and their candle shall be put out (Prov. 24:20). Because to be worldly minded is death, but to be spiritually minded is life and peace, and if anyone does not have the Spirit of God, they do not belong to God (Rom. 8:5–10). We must abstain from fleshly lust that war against the soul (1 Pet. 2:11). "The human spirit is willing, but the flesh is weak" (Matt. 26:41). But if you allow Christ to do so, he will strengthen and settle you (1 Pet. 5:6–11; Ps. 3:5; 55:22).

SOME PEOPLE BELIEVE & CONFESS BUT ARE FULL OF THE DEVIL

There was a female in the Bible who was a worker of witchcraft, voodoo, sorcery, and black magic and she made plenty of money for people. She confessed with her mouth the Lord Jesus Christ and believed in her heart that God raised Christ from the dead, but she was possessed with a demon, so not everyone who confesses Christ is of Christ, but a lot of people are of the devil (Acts 16:16-24). People who sin are of the devil because sin is not of God, but of the devil (1 John 3:5-10; Prov. 11:31; 1 Pet. 4:18).

Not everyone who sins is possessed with a demon or the devil, but some people are possessed and do not know it" (Matt. 12:43-45; 2 Pet. 2:19). When you acknowledge the true Word of God, it is good if you can profess it while living a godly life. To confess is to simply speak, but to profess means to do, like when a person has a profession that earns them a paycheck (Titus 1:1). We should be doers of the Word of God (James 1:22-27; Matt. 13:1-23; Acts 17:11-12; Ps. 81:10-16; Jer. 15:15-21; Rev. 10:9-11).

John 3:15-21 says that God gave his only begotten Son, that whosoever believes in him should not perish, but have eternal life, and that Christ did not come to condemn the world, but to save it, and that they who do not believe are condemned. But the Bible also says that Christ is the light of the world (John 1:1-14;

8:12). And that people love darkness rather than light, and their love of darkness and sin shall condemn them (John 3:15–21). If you say you fear God and that you obey his voice, but you still walk in darkness, then you must reevaluate yourself (Isa. 50:10; 2 Kings 17:20–41). People who confess Christ must also keep his commandments (Dan. 9:4). Bible scripture says, "Let my heart be blameless regarding your Word, so I will not be ashamed" (Ps. 119:80).

CONFESSING CHRIST WHILE BEING AN OPPRESSOR & HIGH-MINDED

We cannot be right with God in our heart if our hearts are not right toward all people, all races, all socioeconomic statuses, all social classes, and with pets and animals (1 John 2:9–11; 3:13–15; 4:20; Prov. 12:10).

FEARING GOD CAUSES FORGIVENESS

God has mercy on us all, but he has more mercy on people who fear him (Luke 1:50). The Lord is near people who call upon him in truth and who fear and love him (Ps. 66:16–20; 115:11; 130:3–4; 145:17–21).

God's forgiveness toward us is meant to cause us to love and fear him, not simply believe, confess, and call upon him as a weak Christian or a hypocrite (Ps. 66:16–20; 130:3–4; 145:17–21). Blessed is everyone who fears the Lord. Their spouses and children shall be beneficial to them (Ps. 128). They who fear the Lord must also trust in the Lord, and he will bless those who fear him, both small and great, and their children (Ps. 115:11–18). The mercy of the Lord is forever on people who fear him, and on their grandchildren, when God's Word is obeyed (Ps. 103:13, 17–18). As a parent has pity on their children, the Lord has pity on people who fear him (Ps. 103:13). God says in the Old Testament that he has mercy on people who love him and keep his commandments (Exod. 20:6). And Christ says in the New Testament that we are his friends only if we do whatever he commands us to do (John 14:15; 15:14–15). We must live in the fear of God and in the comfort of the Holy Ghost (Acts 9:31). The Bible says that we begin to be wise when we learn to fear God (Ps. 111:10). The Bible also teaches us to ask God to establish his Word in us as servants and that we must be devoted to fearing God (Ps. 119:33–38). We must be servants of the Lord and not simply beneficiaries. We must be God's servants because he is not our servant. Therefore, if all we must do to be saved is believe in our heart that God raised Christ from the dead and confess that truth with our mouth, then why does the Bible also say that we must both love and fear the Lord (Luke 1:50; Deut. 5:10; 7:9; 13:4; Heb. 12:26-29; Ps. 66:16-20; 130:3-4; 145:17-21; Prov.16:6; Lev. 26:3-6; Dan. 9:3-19)?

Solomon prayed to the Lord and said, When the heavens are shut up and there is no rain because the people have sinned, when they pray and confess your name, and turn from their sin because you afflict them, then hear in heaven, and forgive the sin of your people, that you may teach them the good way in which they should walk, and send rain on your land which you have given to your people. When there is famine, disease, loss of crops, enemies, and sickness, and they pray with their hands speeded towards you, hear, answer, and forgive them according to their ways and according to their heart, that they may fear you all the days that they live. (1 Kings 8:33-40) God answers our prayers according to the idols in our heart, and idolatry is forbidden by God (Ezek. 14:1-11; 23:49; 1 Cor. 10:14; Gal. 5:19-26; Col. 3:5; 1 Sam. 15:23).

God takes pleasure in people who fear him and hope in his mercy (Ps. 119:132; 147:10-11). Therefore, although we must be wise enough to fear God, we all need mercy sometimes, and that is why David loved the Lord and expressed it repeatedly when he wrote the book of Psalms, but scripture also says that David feared the Lord (1 Chron. 21:27-30). In every nation, people who fear God and work righteousness are accepted by God (Acts 10:35). God is good and does good, and we should ask him to teach us his ways (Ps. 119:64-72). David asked the Lord, "Teach me your ways, so I will talk of your wondrous works. Remember, O Lord, your tender mercies, and your lovingkindness. For they have been from long ago" (Ps. 25:4-10; 119:12, 26, 33, 64, 66, 108, 124).

To people who obey God, they shall receive eternal life, glory, honor, and peace and there is no respect of persons with God, because we reap what we sow (Rom. 2:4-11; Gal. 6:7-10). When we tell people too often that God is good and that he forgives us, that does not cause most people to live right (Rom. 2:4–6; Isa. 57:10–11). Certain people in the Old Testament did not serve God wholeheartedly after he warned, punished, and destroyed millions of them (Isa. 1:5–9; 2 Kings 17; Hag. 2:17). And even though the pharaoh sinned more after he experienced God's punishment in the days of Moses, God still had the last word (Exod. 9:33–35). We must tell people how good, gracious, merciful, and long-suffering God is and warn them about his wrath and displeasure with our sinful ways. People do not have a problem believing that God forgives us, because if Christ had not died for our sins, we would have been dead a long time ago. Maybe people tell other people about the goodness of God more than they tell them about the wrath or displeasure of God because sometimes it seems as though God is not near while they are suffering or feeling alone. But God is always in control, and not even a single bird falls from the sky without God doing it or allowing it (Matt. 10:28–31; Luke 12:6–7). God hears our cry and is long-suffering while he waits for us to finally repent, so we must be long-suffering and faithful toward him while we wait on him (Luke 18:7–8; Isa. 42:14). Love suffers long (1 Cor. 13:4). None of us suffers longer than Christ. When Christ suffered, he committed himself to God, and so should we (1 Pet. 2:19–25). By God's mercy and truth, our sins are forgiven, but we must depart from sin because we also fear God (Prov. 16:6). When God holds his peace through grace and punishes us lightly, that does not cause some people to fear him (Rom. 2:4–6; Isa. 57:10–11). Most people want to hear that God is good and that he does not punish us. However, God himself says that his goodness toward us does not cause us to fear or obey him, but that it should (Isa. 57:11–13; Hosea 3:5). God says he will forgive our sins and cleanse us of our sinful acts if we allow him to do so, and when people hear the good that God does toward us, they shall fear God for his goodness and the prosperity that he provides (Jer. 33:8–9). God is good, but that same good God will send many people to hell. God is good, but how good are you to God? On judgment day, God will say to you, "Well done, my good and faithful servant" (Matt. 25:23). And you shall receive a crown of life because those of us who are with Christ even in hard times are called, chosen, and faithful (Rev. 2:10; 17:14). On the other hand, God will say to people who call on the Lord and who confess his name but still live in sin and iniquity, "Depart from me, you worker of iniquity" (Luke 13:22–30; Matt. 7:21–23). We must love, trust, and fear God and not just simply love him for his goodness (Heb. 12:26–29; Isa. 66:1–2; Deut. 5:29; Exod. 20:20; Ps. 115:11; Prov. 22:4; 23:17; Mal. 2:5–6).

FAITH WITHOUT WORKS IS DEAD & BELIEVING WITHOUT OBEYING IS DEAD

To believe is to accept as true, to commit, and to have faith (John 20:30–31). For yet a little while, Christ who shall come will come and not wait any longer (Heb. 6:1–6; 10:35–39; 11:1, 6; Luke 18:1–8).

To believe is to have faith, and to have faith is to believe. But faith and belief without works is dead and meaningless, and faith without good works cannot save you (James 2:13–26). The just shall live by faith, and it is impossible to please God without faith (Rom. 1:16–18; Hab. 2:4; Gal. 3:11), for we walk by faith, not by sight (2 Cor. 5:7). If anyone draws back or backslides, God has no pleasure in them (Heb. 10:38; Rom. 1:16–18; Hab. 2:4; Gal. 3:11).

Therefore, let us draw near Christ with a true heart. Let us hold fast the profession of our faith without wavering, having been washed with pure water in baptism, for Christ is faithful who promised us all things, even eternal life. Let us love one another and do good works toward all people, not forgetting to assemble and to warn one another even more as judgment day, our dying day, and as our birthdays approach (Heb. 10:22–25).

BEING TOO STUBBORN OR TOO SICK TO CALL ON THE LORD

It is best to live right and call on the name of the Lord daily with a pure heart while following righteousness, faith, love, and peace, fleeing youthful lusts (2 Tim. 2:22; Job 27:8–23; Prov. 3:5–8).

After we believe in our heart and confess with our mouth, a sinful heart must depart from us (Ps. 101:3-4). Some people cannot call on Christ because they are presently doing something sinful. And some people did not have time to call on the Lord before death because they died suddenly. And yet others are too hard-hearted and stubborn to call on the Lord while they are on their deathbed. But for people in trouble who call on the Lord, God is merciful and gracious to save their soul and their body, and if they should still die, they could go to heaven, which is the ultimate goal (Rom. 8:26–34).

Calling on Christ can indeed save you, but unless we are too ill, mentally, or physically, to serve the Lord, simply calling on Christ may not save us. And people who are too sick to call on the Lord for themselves, if they were already a saved saint of God, the Holy Ghost prays for them with heavenly groanings that we do not understand on earth. God who searches the heart knows what the mind of the Holy Spirit is because the Holy Spirit makes intercessions for the saints according to the will of

God. All things work together for the good of people who love God and are called according to his purpose, and God justifies and glorifies them as saints (Rom. 8:26–30). Therefore, those wonderful scriptures do not pertain to just any person who called on the name of the Lord before they became sick. Also, God hardens whom he will and has mercy on whom he will, so some terminally ill people will receive mercy, while others will not repent because God hardens their heart, mainly because he knows that they will not repent anyway, or that God has already made up his mind to send them to hell (Rom. 9:11, 14–21; Exod. 9:12–18; 10:27; 14:8; 33:19; Ps. 105:24–45; Prov. 21:1; Isa. 24:1–3; 63:16–19; Josh. 11:16–20; Matt. 20:1–16; Zech. 10:6; Gen. 19:12–25; John 9:39 – 41).

GRACE DOES NOT MEAN THAT WE SHOULD BE A SLAVE TO SIN

The Bible says, "Shall we sin willfully because we are under grace? God forbids" (Rom. 6:1–3). We are justified by Christ, but Christ is not the minister of sin (Gal. 2:17). God asks, what sin have people found in him that causes them to sin (Jer. 2:5)? "Know ye not that you are slaves to whomever you obey, whether of sin unto death, or of obedience unto righteousness? God be thanked, that you were the servants and slaves of sin, but you have obeyed from the heart the truth that has been delivered unto you" (Rom. 6:15–17; 1 John 5:14–17; Rev. 3:15–19; Matt. 12:33; Ps. 66:16–20).

The key words are "heart" and "obeyed." If you build again the sin that you turned away from, you make yourself a sinner again (Gal. 2:16–18). If you live in darkness after confessing Christ, you lie to yourself and do not practice the truth (1 John 1:6). If we say we know Christ and do not obey his Word, we are liars. People who say they abide in the Lord ought to live as Christ lived (1 John 2:4). Do not receive the grace of God in vain, nor take grace for granted (2 Cor. 6:1–10). The Bible tells us to be strong in the grace that is in Christ Jesus and not to be weak in Christ's grace (2 Tim. 2:1). Grace does not allow us to sin (Jude 1:4). God says, "Let us have grace," but we must still serve God acceptably with reverence and godly fear, because our God is a consuming fire and a jealous God (Heb. 12:28–29; Deut. 4:24). No one can see God without holiness, and we can fail the grace of God (Heb. 12:14–15; Rom. 12:1–2; 2 Tim. 2:15).

OBEDIENCE IS BETTER THAN SACRIFICE

Obedience is better than sacrifice, unless we offer the sacrifice of righteousness and put our trust in the Lord (1 Sam. 15:22; Rom. 12:1 – 2; Matt. 9:10 – 13; 23:23; Prov. 21:3; Ps. 4:5; 40:6 – 8: Hos. 6:6; Mic. 6:7; Heb. 13:15).

To make sacrifices such as giving to the church and to the poor, for example, but continuing to live in sin, those kinds of sacrifices are not better than obedience to the Lord. Jesus was obedient and a sacrifice as well, including not only when he suffered and died but also when he left his riches in heaven to live in poverty on earth for our sake (2 Cor. 8:9; Phil. 4:19; Lev. 12:6–8; Luke 2:21–24; Rom. 15:1–3).

SATAN BELIEVES AND CONFESSES BUT SATAN ALSO FEARS GOD

Some people say that all you must do to be saved is to confess and believe. Satan confesses and believes that Jesus is the Son of God, but Satan trembles at the name of Jesus, and so should we (James 2:18–20; Mark 1:23–24; 3:11–12; Luke 10:17).

Satan is more powerful than most humans, who should also fear God (Eph. 6:11–17; Isa. 66:1–2). After hearing the Apostle Paul, Felix trembled, but he told Paul that he would talk to him later (Acts 24:25–26). When you believe, you must also speak the truth (2 Cor. 4:13).

THE DEVIL IS THE FATHER OF HABITUAL, REBELLIOUS AND WILLFUL SINNERS

Although Jesus was accused of having a demon, he was never possessed with a demon (John 8:48–49; 14:30). But Satan did try to tempt Christ, to no avail (Luke 4:1–13). Jesus says that he did nothing of himself, but he did only what he saw his Father do (John 5:19). Christ says that he speaks that which he has seen in his Father, and sinners and hypocrite Christians do those things that they have seen in their father, the devil, and the lusts of the devil they will do, because they are of the devil and are not of God (John 8:34–47; 1 Tim. 5:15; 1 John 3:5–10; Prov. 11:31; 1 Pet. 4:18).

GOD TESTS THE HEART, SO BE CAREFUL HOW YOU CLAIM TO HAVE A GOOD HEART

If living a righteous life is not important, why did God say that people who influenced many others to live right shall shine like stars when they get to heaven (Dan. 12:1–4; Prov. 11:30)?

God says in the Old and New Testaments that he tries the heart (Jer. 11:20; 1 Thess. 2:4). Because the heart can be deceitful above all things and desperately wicked, therefore the Lord searches our heart (Jer. 17:9–11). God knows the secrets of the heart (Ps. 44:20–21; 2 Chron. 6:30).

God knows the imaginations and thoughts of the heart. God will bring to light the counsels of the heart when he comes (1 Chron. 28:9; 1 Cor. 4:5), because most people's ways are right in their own eyes, but God examines the heart (Prov. 21:2). The Hebrews while leaving slavery in Egypt returned to Egypt in their hearts (Acts 7:38–39). The Lord says that he searches the heart and inner body, and he gives unto everyone according to their works (Rev. 2:21–26; Jer. 17:9–11; 21:14; 32:19; 1 Kings 2:44).

Sooner or later, Christ will try you to see if your heart can stand for all the Word of God, because we must live by every

Word of God (Luke 4:1–4; Exod. 24:7; Deut. 4:1–9; 8:2–3).

Thus, we must do more than simply believe, confess, and call on the name of the Lord (Rom. 10:9, 13). Even if we cannot obey every Word of God, we must accept the entire Word of God and stand for and support every Word of God and not reject it or support antibiblical laws, practices, and lifestyles. Christ was tested by God in the wilderness and God allowed the devil to tempt Christ, but Christ quoted scripture when he rebuked the devil (Luke 4:1–4). And God led the Hebrews in the wilderness to humble them and allowed them to hunger to test their heart, whether they would keep his commandments or not, and to teach them that they must not live by food and earthly possessions alone, but by every Word of God (Deut. 8:2–3; Luke 4:1–4).

There is a generation that is pure in its own eyes but is not washed from its filthiness (Prov. 21:2; 30:12; Deut. 12:8). The Bible says, "Do good, O Lord, to those who are good, and to those who have a righteous heart" (Ps. 125:4–5). To hypocrites, habitual and willful sinners, to atheists, and to anti-Christians, the Word of God says, "As silver, brass, iron, and tin is gathered into the furnace to melt it, so will I gather you in my anger and in my fury, and I will leave you there, and melt you" (Ezek. 22:20). The refiner is for silver and the furnace for gold, but the Lord tests the heart to see if it is pure and if it can stand God's tests, like refiners and furnaces test silver and gold (Prov. 17:3). Christ says that they who come to him must worship him in spirit and in truth (John 4:23–24; Zech. 8:1–8). God desires truth in the inward parts of our body, the heart (Ps. 51:6). God's Word is truth, and we must be sanctified through the truth (John 17:17, 19; Col. 1:5–6; 1 Thess. 2:13). Christ gives eternal salvation to people who obey him (Heb. 5:7–9). God gives the Spirit of truth, which is the Holy Ghost, to people who obey him, and the Holy Ghost strengthens us (Acts 5:32; Luke 11:13; John 14:13–18, 26–27).

God tries the heart, and he has pleasure in people who are righteous (1 Chron. 29:17). Trust in the Lord with all your heart and lean not to your own understanding. In all your ways acknowledge him, and he shall direct your paths. Be not wise in your own eyes, fear the Lord, and depart from evil. It shall be health to your navel, and marrow to your bones (Prov. 3:5–8; 2 Chron. 31:21; Num. 15:39–41; Jer. 29:11–13).

The navel in this scripture also indicates the inner being and the heart (Prov. 3:5–8). The Bible also says that the Word of God is sharper than any two-edged sword, cutting deep into the bone marrow, soul, and spirit and is a discerner of the thoughts and intents of the heart (Heb. 4:12). The book of Psalms tells us that when our hearts are not right with God, his blessings are limited, and we could be faced with years of trouble and even death (Ps. 78:32–41). What is in your heart will come out, whether it is God, self, or the devil (Matt. 12:34; 15:15–20; John 2:24–25; Ps. 51:1–6; Prov. 23:6–7; Jer. 17:9–10; Isa. 59:12; 1 Cor. 2:4; 1 Thess. 1:5).

WHAT IS IN YOUR HEART WILL COME OUT

God told the prophet Ezekiel to listen to him carefully and to take his word to heart (Ezek. 3:10). Where your treasure is, so will your heart be also, whether that treasure is heaven, good things, or sinful things (Matt. 6:19–21, 24–33; 19:16–30; Rom. 2:6–11; Phil. 2:21; Heb. 11:24–27).

Christ says that we must love him with all our heart, all our soul, and with all our mind (Matt. 22:37–39; Deut. 6:5). The Bible tells us, "Rejoice young people, in the time of your youth, and let your heart be joyful in your youth, and walk in the ways of your heart, and in the sight of your eyes. But know, that for all these things, God will bring you into judgment" (Eccles. 11:9; 12:13–14; Rom. 2:16).

Every idle word that we speak shall be judged by God, and our spoken words justify us or condemn us, just as hypocritically confessing Christ with our mouth condemns us (Matt. 12:36–37). Before Christ died for all people, God choose the ancient Israelites, ancient Jews, and ancient Hebrews unto himself to be a holy people, separate from the rest of the world (1 Kings 8:53; Exod. 19:5; Deut. 14:2; 26:18; Ps. 135:4; Titus 2:14; 1 Pet. 2:9; 1 John 2:2; Acts 17:26; Heb. 2:9; Rom. 5:6–9; 8:32; Isa. 53).

Not only did God eventually accept and bless all nations, but he also said that all nations will be punished with ancient Israel, because those nations were unholy, but ancient Israel was unholy in the heart and resisted the Holy Ghost (Jer. 9:25–26;

Acts 7:51). God wants to put a new spirit in us, replace the stony and hard heart, and give us a spiritual heart of flesh, that we may walk in his Word, keep his Word, and be doers of his Word, and we shall be his people, and he shall be our God (Ezek. 11:19–20; 36:23–27). Remember, we must be doers of the Word and not just hearers (James 1:22–27; Matt. 13:1–23; Acts 17:11–12; Ps. 81:10–16; Jer. 15:15–21; Rev. 10:9–11).

The lamp of the body is the eye. Therefore, when your eye is good, your whole body is full of light, but when your eye is unholy, your body also is full of darkness and evil (Luke 11:33–36). Jesus says, if your hand, foot, or eyes cause you to sin, spiritually cut them off, because it is better to live a life without hands, feet, and eyes than to have your whole body cast into hell (Matt. 18:8–9). What is in you will come out, whether it is good or bad (Isa. 59:12; 1 Cor. 2:4; 1 Thess. 1:5; Matt. 12:34; 15:15–20; Ps. 51:1–6; Prov. 23:6–7; 27:19; 1 Sam. 24:13).

WE MUST SUFFER LIKE CHRIST & NOT LIKE A SINNER

We must not join the body of Christ only for blessings, but to also be Christlike, which means we must also suffer like him and carry our own cross, or we cannot be his disciple (Luke 14:26–27; Deut. 33:9). The Bible says, "We should have confidence in the day of judgment, as he is, so are we in this world" (1 John 4:17). And just as an African man helped Jesus carry his physical cross, Christ will help you carry your cross of adversity, affliction, persecution, sickness, and suffering but you must live and sometimes suffer like Christ (Mark 15:21). Christ suffered for us, leaving us an example, that we should follow his steps (1 Pet. 2:21). We are the children of God only when we obey him and when we are holy, sanctified, and separate from the world (Acts 5:32; Luke 11:13; John 14:13–18, 26–27; Phil. 2:15; 1 Pet. 1:13–17; Rom. 8:1, 5–14; 2 Cor. 6:17–18; Deut. 32:4–5).

Christ says whoever obeys him is his mother, brother, and sister (Matt. 12:46–50; Mark 3:31–35). Also, being children of God, if we want to share Christ's glory, we must also share his suffering (Rom. 8:16–17). And we must be obedient and holy (Acts 5:32; Luke 11:13; John 14:13–18, 26–27; 1 Pet. 1:13–17).

Most people seek their own desires and not the things that are of Jesus Christ (Phil. 2:21; 1 Tim. 6:9–10; James 3:13–16; John 5:41, 44; 1 Cor. 13:5).

The Apostle Paul chose to live and suffer like Christ, and he said, "Things that were gain to me, I counted as a loss for Christ's sake. And I count all things as a loss for the excellency of the knowledge of Christ Jesus my Lord, for whom I have suffered the loss of all things, and count them as dung, that I may win Christ. Not having my own righteousness, but the righteousness that is of God by faith, that I may know him, and the fellowship of his suffering" (Phil. 3:7–11; 2 Tim. 1:12).

While Job was suffering, his wife told him to curse God and die to end his suffering, but to curse God is a sin that resulted in immediate death in the Old Testament (Lev. 24:10–15, 23). Job told his wife and friends that we must not expect only good from God and that although it seemed like God was killing him, Job said, "Yet will I still trust in him" (Job 2:8–10; 13:15–16). Before God tried and tested Job's heart by making him sick, killing his children, and destroying his wealth, Job prayed regularly for his children's safety, but God still tested his heart by killing his children (Job 1:1–5).

To be afflicted or to face adversity from God can sometimes be a blessing, as was the case with David. He said that it was good that he was afflicted so he could learn God's ways (Ps. 119:71). Jeremiah said that his ministry caused him to receive affliction from God because of God's wrath on other people and that his affliction made his skin, flesh, and bones feel old (Lam. 3:1–4). Jesus witnessed a good confession while he was being tried and crucified before Pontius Pilate, and Jesus instructs us to keep his commandment without spot, unrebukable, until his return (1 Tim. 6:13–14). David was a king, and he at one point committed terrible sins, but he repented and lived a sanctified and holy life, being a new creature, and being once again first with God (2 Sam. 11; 12:1–24; 15; 1 Kings 3:6; 14:8; 15:3–5).

David wrote, "God rewarded me according to my righteousness and the cleanness of my hands. I have kept the ways of the Lord and have not wickedly departed from my God. I am also blameless before him, and I have kept myself from iniquity. God will save his afflicted people, but he brings down high looks" (Ps. 18:20–27). The same applies to the church of God because Christ is returning for a church without spot, wrinkle, or blemish (Eph. 5:1–28; 1 Pet. 1:13–19; 2 Pet. 3:1–14; 1 Tim. 6:3–16; Jude 1:22–24).

True religion according to the Bible is to go unspotted from the world and to help the fatherless and the widow in their affliction (James 1:26–27; Isa. 1:15 – 20). Christ says to not only believe in him, but also to suffer for his sake (Phil. 1:29). So as you can see, to "believe" also means to "obey" Jesus and live a sanctified and righteous life, separated from willful sin (John 17:17–19; Isa. 29:23; Heb. 4:14–16; 10:26; Mic. 2:1; Ps. 19:12–14; Rom. 1:18–32; 2 Thess. 2:10–15).

SOME PEOPLE GO TO HELL AFTER BELIEVING, CONFESSING & CALLING ON CHRIST

Not everyone who says, "Lord, Lord," shall enter the kingdom of heaven, but they who do the will of God shall go to heaven (Matt. 7:21-23; Mic. 3:11). Blessed are they who always practice righteousness" (Ps. 106:3; 119:20). Some people flatter God with their mouth and lie to him with their tongue (Ps. 78:36). We must receive the Word of God in our hearts after we hear it, and people usually do what is in their heart, because where your treasure is, there shall your heart be too (Ezek. 3:10; Luke 12:32-34; Rom. 2:6-11; 1 Kings 3:7-15; Heb. 11:24-27).

Jesus told Nicodemus that we must be born again of the water and of the Spirit, or we cannot go to heaven (John 3:1-7). The Bible says, "If we sin willfully after we have received the knowledge of the truth, there remains no more sacrifice for sins, but there is only a fearful expectation of judgment and fiery punishment. They who broke Moses' law died without mercy under two or three witnesses, how much sorer punishment for those who have trodden underfoot the Son of God, and counted his sanctified blood an unholy thing, and did it despite the Spirit of grace? It is a fearful thing to fall into the hands of the living

God." (Heb. 10:26–31; Exod. 20:18–19; Deut. 5:23–26; Mic. 2:1; Ps. 19:12–14).

Remember, the people in Moses's time begged to hear Moses after initially rebelling against Moses, because if God had spoken to them, they knew they would have surely died (Exod. 20:18–19; Deut. 5:23–26).

The Holy Scripture says, "God's voice shook the earth in the Old Testament, but during these last and evil days, he will shake heaven and earth, because God is a consuming fire, and a jealous God, whose name is Jealous" (Deut. 4:24; Exod. 34:14; Heb. 12:26–29).

When we believe, we must also believe that there is a heaven being prepared for us (John 14:1–4) and that God could destroy us and send us to hell if we do not obey him, because scripture says that God is faithful to do good toward us (1 Thess. 5:24; Isa. 11:4–5; Deut. 7:9; Ps. 31:21–24).

Scripture also says that God is faithful to send sinners to hell (Rev. 20:5–8), because when God says it, he will do it (Isa. 46:9–10; 55:11; Jer. 23:20; Ezek. 24:13–14). The Bible even says, "Whoso is wise, and will observe God's mercy, goodness, and his punishments, they shall understand the lovingkindness of the Lord" (Ps. 107). Unwise people do not think that God can be good, merciful, and terrible too; but the Bible tells us that in his punishing wrath, God can be terrible (Exod. 34:10; Deut. 7:21; 10:17; Neh. 1:5; 4:14; 9:32; Job 37:22; Ps. 47:2; Jer. 20:11).

Destruction from God happened with the ancient Israelites in the wilderness and with the people of Noah's day, and in Sodom and Gomorrah when even angels were destroyed because they did not believe that God would do it (2 Pet. 2:1–9; Jude 1:5–7; Rev. 12:9). The Holy Scripture also says that people did not believe Moses and the prophets, and some people nowadays will not believe that they can go to hell even if someone returned from hell today to warn them (Luke 16:19–31; Acts 13:41). Christ returned from heaven to warn the earth while simultaneously saving the souls of people, healing them, and delivering them. Christ even asked one man how he can believe heavenly things if he did not even believe what Christ said about earthly things (John 3:12–13). Judgment day, which is for most people, the day that we die, because we will rise from the dead in the same sinful or righteous condition that we were in when we lived (Rev. 22:10–13).

WE MUST BE CHRIST – LIKE ON EARTH TO BE LIKE CHRIST IN HEAVEN

When we get to heaven, we shall see God like he is, and we shall be like him (Phil. 3:17–21; 1 John 3:2; Ps. 17:14–15). But we cannot be like him in heaven if we do not strive to be like him on earth (Titus 2:11–12; Matt. 6:10; 1 Cor. 6:9–11; 1 Tim. 6:9–10; 2 Kings 5:15–27).

When God walked the earth in the human body of Christ, God said and is still saying to the entire world that he will not ask us to do or to suffer anything that he did not experience himself, but yet without sinning himself (Heb. 2:16–18; 4:14–16; Num. 23:19; 1 John 3:5; Ps. 92:15; 1 Pet. 2:21–23; Gal. 2:17).

We were made in the image of God, and we must retain that image while we live (Isa. 43:7, 20–22; Gen. 1:26; 1 Cor. 11:7; 15:47–55; Phil. 2:6–11; James 3:9).

GOD DOES NOT HEAR THE PRAYERS, CALLS & CRYING OF SOME PEOPLE

God says that sometimes before we call, he will answer, and while we are yet speaking, he will hear, but this is mainly in reference to righteous people (Isa. 65:24). God does hear the prayers, crying, and calling of sinners too, but only regarding earthly help and necessities, because the Bible says that God does not hear the prayers of sinners when it comes to repentance, unless they are truly repenting wholeheartedly (Job 8:20; 35:13; Prov. 1:28–30; Jer. 14:7–12; Mal. 2:17; John 9:24–33).

David said, "I cried unto God with my mouth. If I regard sin in my heart, the Lord will not hear me. But God has heard me, he has attended to the voice of my prayer. Blessed be God who has not turned away my prayer, nor his mercy from me" (Ps. 66:16–20). God told Job's friends that he would hear Job's prayers, but not their prayers (Job 4:1–8; 32:1–10; 34:34–37; 42:7–9).

Some people do not feel that they must repent because they think they are not doing anything wrong or that their wrong is not as bad as other people's. But God says, "I listened and heard, but they do not speak right, no one repented of their sin and wickedness, and they say, 'What have I done?' Everyone turns to their own way of doing things" (Jer. 8:6). Some people do not pray, repent, or call on the name of the Lord until they are in trouble or when God chastises them (Isa. 26:16; 1 Kings 8:32–

40). The Lord said by the mouth of Isaiah, "God's hand is not shortened that it cannot save, neither is his ear closed that it cannot hear, but your sins have separated you from God, and he will not hear your prayers" (Isa. 59:1–4; 64:4–8; Ps. 107:17–22; Mal. 2:2; Hosea 14:1). Just as God did not answer the prayers of King Saul anymore because of sin (1 Sam. 28:6). God told the Prophet Jeremiah, "I know the thoughts that I think towards you, thoughts of peace, and not of evil, to give you an expected end. Then shall you call upon me, and pray unto me, and I will hearken unto you. And you shall seek me and find me when you search for me with your whole heart" (Jer. 29:11–14). But notice that God had already punished those people very hard (Jer. 29:10).

So, as you can see, believing in your heart, confessing Christ with your mouth, and calling on the name of the Lord is not all we must do to be saved; but you must do those things in righteousness or at least start trying to live right after doing those things. Talk is cheap. To clarify even further, the Bible says that there is a sin unto death and that people should not pray about it. And there is a sin not unto death, and people should indeed pray about it (1 John 5:16–19). When we pretend to repent, God does not hear those prayers, and those sins can cause us to die in sin, but when we repent sincerely and wholeheartedly, God hears us and that is the sin not unto death (1 John 5:16–19; Jer. 7:16–20; 11:14; 14:11; Rev. 3:15–19; Matt. 12:33; Rom. 6:15–17).

Sinners who humble themselves and admit their wrong even if they do not have the strength to turn away from their sins are more likely to be heard and answered by God than sinners who say that God forgives us for everything while proudly living in sin (Luke 18:9–14; 23:39–46). God, in his grace and mercy, blesses ungodly people, and some of them still make plans against him (Hosea 7:15). But people who strive to live righteously always are favored by God, their prayers are heard at all times even if they do not get the answer that they want, and they will also inherit eternal life (Ps. 106:3; 119:20). Jesus says that if you forsake all and follow him, you shall receive in return a hundred times that which you lost in this life but expect persecutions on earth, followed by eternal life in heaven (Mark 10:28–31; Job 1; 2:1–10; 13:15–16; 42; 1 Cor. 7:25–34; Luke 14:25–27, 33).

When Jesus healed and delivered sinners in the Bible, he told them to go and sin no more or a worse thing will happen to them (John 5:14; 8:3–11). If after people escape the pollutions of the world and become entangled again in the world, their latter end will be worse than the beginning (2 Pet. 2:20; 1 John 5:4–5). The way of a sinner is hard (Prov. 13:15; Jer. 40:3; 44:23).

IT WILL BE TOO LATE TO CALL ON GOD ON JUDGMENT DAY

It was made very clear in the book of Acts that Jesus was sent to save and bless us and that we are to repent, turn away from our sins, and be converted or that same Jesus could destroy us (Acts 3:19–26). And Jesus himself says that he will not hear sinners on judgment day and that there will be weeping and grinding of teeth (Matt. 8:11–12; 13:38–43; Luke 13:24–28).

On judgment day, the Bible says, "They who are holy and righteous shall still be holy and righteous, and they who are filthy and unrighteous shall still be filthy and unrighteous. It will be too late to call on the Lord." Furthermore, Christ says, "I come quickly, and my reward is with me, to give to everyone according to their works" (Rev. 22:10–13; Acts 24:15; 1 Pet. 3:18; Dan. 12:1–3; Ezek. 18:19–32; 2 Thess. 1:4–12).

CHRIST IS ASHAMED OF PEOPLE WHO ARE ASHAMED TO CRY OUT UNTO HIM

Jesus says that people who do not openly acknowledge him and openly stand for the truth on earth, he will not stand for them before his Father in heaven and that he will be ashamed of them before God (Mark 8:38; Matt. 10:32–33). We must not even be ashamed to confess and call on the name of Christ in the presence of kings and other politicians (Ps. 119:46–47; Jude 1:3). God blesses us in the presence of our enemies and nonbelievers, and we must likewise stand for his Word and bless Christ in their presence (Ps. 23; 31:19; 1 Pet. 3:15). "Be steadfast, unmovable, always abounding in the work of the Lord, knowing that your work is not in vain in the Lord" (1 Cor. 15:58). The Apostle Paul was chosen to suffer great things for Christ's name before the ancient Jews, Gentiles, kings, and politicians (Acts 9:10–16). The Bible says, "The Lord is on my side, I will not fear. What can humans do to me? The Lord is for me. Therefore, I shall see my desire on those who hate me. It is better to trust in the Lord than to put confidence in mankind and in politicians" (Ps. 56:4; 118:6–9). Blessed are they who are not offended in Christ (Matt. 11:6). And when Christ delivers people and sets them free from sin, sickness, bad habits, and bondage and afterwards they return to their sinful lifestyle, they crucify Christ over again and put him to an open shame (Heb. 6:1–6).

YOUR HEART SHALL BE WHERE YOUR VALUES ARE

The Bible says, "If you are currently risen with Christ, seek those things which are above, where Christ sits on the right hand of God. Set your affections on things above, not on things on the earth" (Col. 3:1–2). "The way of life is above to the wise, that they may depart from hell beneath" (Prov. 15:24). The Bible says, "Where your treasure is, there shall your heart be also" (Matt. 6:19–21, 24–33; 19:16–30; Rom. 2:6–11; Phil. 2:21; Heb. 11:24–27).

If your treasure is in heaven, there shall your heart presently be also, and your soul will be there in the future for eternity (Matt. 6:21). But if your treasure is sinful, you and your heart shall be among those sinful things. Many people seek their own desires and not the things that are of Jesus Christ (Phil. 2:21; James 3:13–16). God told one hardworking man that he would die, because the man pursued earthly possessions and was not equally rich toward God (Luke 12:16–21; Isa. 40:21–25). If your actions and heart are right with God, putting God first, you are safe with God, but even if your actions are right and ungodly things are in your heart, God answers your prayers according to those things in your heart that you put before him, which is idolatry (Ezek. 14:1–11; 23:49).

SOME PEOPLE DO NOT CRY OUT TO GOD BECAUSE OF FEAR OF LOSING HUMAN FAVOR

Jesus tells us to believe and confess, because some people will try to believe without confessing and without openly praising his name, because they love the praise of mankind more than the praise of God (John 12:42–43). Paul said, "I am not ashamed of the gospel of Christ, for it is the power of God unto the saving of your soul. The just shall live by faith. For the wrath of God is revealed from heaven against all ungodliness and unrighteousness" (Rom. 1:16–18; Hab. 2:4; Gal. 3:11; Heb. 6:1–6; 10:38; Acts 20:19-20, 27; 2 Tim. 1:12).

Romans 10:10 says to believe with the heart unto righteousness and to confess and repent unto salvation. Several versions of the Bible erroneously changed the meaning and wording of the previously mentioned scripture, except the New King James Version and the King James Version, which is also the only Bible that is called the Authorized Version. In support of the original wording and meaning of Romans 10:9–10 of the Authorized King James Version of the Bible, holy scripture says that we must repent unto salvation, or otherwise, we are faced with death (2 Cor. 7:10). Many ministers have been misleading people by telling them that they are saved when they simply confess with their mouth and believe in their heart. Those ministers have blood on their hands from when struggling, physically ill, mentally ill, slaves of sin, wretched, low confidence, low self-esteem, arrogant, or hypocritical people die in their sins while thinking they were saved because a minister told them that all they must do to be saved is confess and believe. Even newcomers to the Christian Faith who want to live right have been deceived by these ministers. All people should read other parts of the Bible as well or the whole Bible if they can find the time and desire to read the whole Word of God because we must live by every Word of God (Luke 4:4; Exod. 24:7; Deut. 4:1–9; 8:3).

Another scripture in the New Testament tells us that some of the ancient Jews and some Gentiles searched the scriptures daily to see if what the apostles wrote was true. Then they "believed" after embracing other parts of the Bible as well (Acts 17:10–12). God, Christ, the prophets, and the apostles taught and wrote a lot more than Romans 10:9–10, 13. Paul said in Titus 1:1 that he acknowledges and confesses the truth, but it is done in godliness. Besides, if you believe in your heart, you should do right, because what is in your heart will come out, good or bad—just as when a person lusts after a married woman in their heart, it is adultery, because he did wrong in his heart (Matt. 5:27–29; 2 Pet. 2:14; Prov. 23:7; Jer. 17:9–11; Exod. 20:17; James 3:13–16).

The Spirit of God and Word of God, which are the same, helps us to discern the unholy thoughts and intentions of the hearts of others (Heb. 4:12; 1 Cor. 12:10; Eph. 6:17).

ASK GOD WHAT ELSE THAT HE WANTS YOU TO DO

God told Ezekiel, "Receive into your heart all my words" (Ezek. 3:10). Expecting to go to heaven after simply confessing, believing, and calling on Christ is like a kid going to school without completing assignments but still expecting to be promoted to the next grade. When Jesus blinded Saul in the New Testament, converted him to the Christian Faith, and later changed his name to Paul, Christ told him, "Arise, be baptized, and wash away your sins, calling on the name of the Lord" (Acts 22:16). Paul believed in his heart, confessed with his mouth, and called on the name of the Lord but he was still baptized (Act 9:20–24). Paul also instantly said, "Lord, what do you want me to do?" (Acts 9:1–6). We must do a lot after we confess with our mouth and believe in our heart.

WE MUST REPENT & LIVE A HOLY & SANCTIFIED LIFE

The Bible says that we must be sanctified after we repent (Acts 26:18) and that all people everywhere must repent (Acts 17:26, 29–31). Sanctified means to be set apart and set aside for holy use (Ps. 4:3–5; Heb. 12:14–15; Rom. 12:1–2; 2 Tim. 2:19–26).

Jesus asked God to, "Sanctify the people through your truth. Your Word is truth. And for their sakes I sanctify myself, that they also might be sanctified through the truth" (John 17:17–19; Isa. 29:23). Do not be ashamed to be sanctified, because God who sanctifies us is not ashamed to call the sanctified his own people (Heb. 2:11; 11:16). But if we are ashamed of Christ and his sanctified Word, then Christ will be ashamed of us before his Father on judgment day (Matt. 10:32–33; 1 Thess. 2:2; 2 Tim. 1:12; Rev. 3:1–6).

It is the will of God what we be sanctified and holy, and sex sins can cause us to not be sanctified (1 Thess. 4:3–8). People who reject this doctrine do not reject mankind who teaches this, but they reject God who commands this (1 Thess. 2:2; 4:3–8; John 17:17–19; Isa. 29:23; Heb. 2:11; 11:16; Matt. 10:32–33; 2 Tim. 1:12; Rev. 3:1–6).

God wants to sanctify you wholly so your whole spirit, soul, and body will be preserved blameless unto the coming of our Lord Jesus Christ (1 Thess. 5:19–23). Jesus told Paul that he would be sent to the Gentiles (Rom. 11:13) and that he would "open their eyes, turn them from darkness to light, and from the power of Satan to God, that they may receive forgiveness of sins, and inheritance with those who are sanctified by faith in Jesus Christ" (Acts 13:45-52; 26:17-18). The Word of God is good if a person uses it righteously. Know this, the law is not made for a righteous person, but for the lawless, disobedient, ungodly, sinners, unholy, profane, murderers, manslayers, whoremongers, sex outside of marriage and premarital sex, liars, the perjured, and anyone else who is contrary to the Word of God (1 Tim. 1:8-10). Peter shamefully used profanity when he denied Jesus and he swore while saying he did not know Jesus (Matt. 26:66-75). But after he repented with tears, he served the Lord in complete sanctification and labored in the Lord until his death (Matt. 26:66-75; John 21:12-19). David also sinned a terrible sin when he took a man's wife, impregnated her, and had her husband killed, and God punished David terribly. But after accepting his punishment and after repenting, David served the Lord in complete sanctification until his death (2 Sam.11; 12:1-24; 15:1-30; 16:5-14, 21-22; 17:15-22; 18; 1 Kings 15:3-5; Ps. 118:18; Isa. 55:3; Acts 13:34).

David and Peter both served the Lord in sanctification before their great sins, and after their great sins, they did not make any more sinful mistakes, and they died in holiness and sanctification (Rev. 22:10-13; Acts 24:15; Dan. 12:1-3; Ezek. 18:19-32; 2 Thess. 1:4-12).

This is one reason that Jesus told people after he healed and delivered them, "Sin no more or a worse thing will happen to you" (John 5:14; 8:3-11; James 5:13-20; 2 Pet. 2:20; Isa. 57:11-12).

So, people nowadays cannot use David and Peter as an example of how God forgives heathens, infidels, anti-Christians, sinners, hypocrites, and evil and wicked people, unless those people become a true servant of the Lord. Jesus says that we are the salt of the earth but that if salt loses its flavor, it is good for nothing and it is thrown out and trodden under the foot of humans (Matt. 5:13), just as vines and branches that do not produce good fruit are cast into the fire (Isa. 5:1-7; Ezek. 15;

19:10–14; Hosea 10:1–2). People should not look at the sins and forgiveness of David and Peter as excuses for sinning while hoping that they receive that same forgiveness, although God will give us the true mercies of David, and of Peter, if we repent (Isa. 55:3; Acts 13:34). But we should try to live like Christ, Enoch, Methuselah, Mordecai, Melchizedek, Noah, Job, Isaiah, Jeremiah, Daniel, Anna, Esther, Ezra, Nehemiah, the Apostle Paul, Elijah, Elisha, John the Baptist, the Apostle John, Joshua, Caleb and certain others. Some of the original twelve apostles cannot be mentioned with the names of the aforementioned people, because even though they walked with Christ and saw the miracles, Judas betrayed Christ and the other ten ran away and forsook Christ when he was arrested (Mark 14:44–50; Matt. 26:66–75). Christ told them that they would forsake him, because he knows everything—past, present, and future—and they told Christ that they would not, but they did (Matt. 26:30–31; Ps. 147:5; Prov. 3:19–20; Deut. 31:14–23). Job's life and how he handled adversity, sickness, suffering, and temptation was one of the best examples in the Bible of how to live a righteous, holy, and sanctified life while accepting God's will. And he remained righteous even after God killed his children, destroyed his wealth, and took away his health with several terminal illnesses and after his wife condemned him to die and told him that his sick breath stank (Job 1; 2; 4:1–8; 13:15–16; 19:17; 24:1–11; 27:1–6; 29; 31; 32:1–10; 34:34–37).

To see what the apostles saw and to live as they lived is a great service on their part, and a lot of Christians are more like the ten apostles and like David who loved the Lord but made terrible mistakes. Ten of the apostles, eleven including Judas, physically walked with the Lord but still did not serve God as wholeheartedly as the prophets of the Old Testament did who never saw God or the Son of God. Jesus told the apostles, "Blessed are they who have not seen and still believe" (John 20:24–31).

Most Christians nowadays have not denied Christ as Peter did or have killed a woman's husband because they desired the husband's wife, but some Christians still have denied Christ or have been anti-Christian in one way or another. And it is true that God will forgive the worst of us, but to not serve Jesus wholeheartedly after we repent is not an option. Jesus says they who he has forgiven for a few sins love him little, but they who have been forgiven for plenty of sins love him much more (Luke 7:40–48). Saul, who was later called Paul, lived an anti-Christian life; but after Jesus converted him, he labored hard for the Lord and never backslid or forsook the Lord like David and Peter did. In his humility, Paul said he was less than all the original apostles, even though he labored more than all of them (1 Cor. 15:9–10). That is because God forgave Paul for a lot of sins, so Paul labored a lot for the Lord after being saved (Luke 7:40–48). King Hezekiah and King Josiah were not as famous as David and Solomon but were much more righteous (2 Kings 18:4–7; 23:25), Josiah being the most righteous. We should try to be like these sanctified people who were living sacrifices and labored for the Lord. God says that he will wash us whiter than snow even though our sins are as red as scarlet and crimson, but he also tells us to put away evil from before his eyes, cease to do evil, and learn to do good and he will reason with us (Isa. 1:16–20; Rev. 7:14). Our reasonable service is to be a living sacrifice unto the Lord, holy and acceptable unto God (Luke 17:7–10; Rom. 12:1; Eccles. 12:13–14; Deut. 10.12–14; Heb. 12:26–29).

As stated earlier, God says to holy and sanctified people who have labored in his name, "I know your works. Behold, I have set before you an open door, and no one can shut it. You have only a little strength remaining, but you still have not denied my name, and you have kept my Word" (Rev. 3:8). Some Christians go to church on a regular basis and are deacons, mothers of the church, and even ministers but they use profane words in their speech. However, the Bible tells us to rid ourselves of anger, wrath, malice, blasphemy, and filthy words and to let all our conversations be holy (Col. 3:8; 1 Pet. 1:15; 2 Pet. 3:10–12; Ps. 19:12–14; 1 Cor. 15:33; Eph. 4:21–32; Isa. 33:15–16; Mal. 2:5–6).

BELIEVING, CONFESSING & CALLING ON GOD MUST INCLUDE BAPTISM

Romans 10:9, 13 says, "If you confess with your mouth the Lord Jesus and believe in your heart that God raised him from the dead, you shall be saved. For whoever calls on the name of the Lord shall be saved." But the Bible also says that people who are his and let everyone who confesses the name of Christ depart from sin (2 Tim. 2:19). Many shall be called, but few shall be chosen (Matt. 20:14–16). No one can see God the Father except they go through God the Son, and no one gets to Christ without living by what the original apostles did and wrote, all of it, not just what is so beautifully and graciously written in the tenth chapter of Romans (John 5:22–23; 14:1, 6; Acts 4:12; Matt. 10:40).

False prophets, hypocrite preachers, and unwise preachers are telling people that all they must do to be saved is believe in their heart and confess with their mouth and they shall be saved (Rom. 10:9, 13). To say that only believing and confessing will save you without living right has become one of the biggest lies in history. A preacher in 2014 said that people do not have to be baptized in the name of Jesus Christ like Peter and Paul commanded (Acts 2:36-39; 8:14-17; 10:42-48; 19:1-6; John 3:3-7).

The preacher said that Peter and Paul were trying to get the ancient Jews to accept Jesus. That same preacher said that we do not have to be baptized at all and that to simply believe and confess the name of the Lord will save us. The truth is that the scriptures speak to all of us and we must fulfill both scriptures to be saved. We must believe, repent, confess, call on God, be baptized in Christ's name, be filled with the Holy Ghost, and continue to believe, confess, and call on the name of Christ (Acts 2:36-41; Rom. 10:1-3, 8-14; 1 Kings 8:33-34).

The Apostle Peter reminded the ancient Jews that whosoever calls on the name of the Lord shall be saved. He then performed the first baptism by baptizing about three thousand people in the name of the Lord Jesus Christ after they repented for their sins (Acts 2:21, 36-47). Jesus says that we cannot go to heaven unless we are born again of the water and of the Holy Spirit (John 3:3-7). The people in Matt. 7:21-23 confessed but did not obey and were cast away by Jesus. Being baptized symbolizes the death, burial, and resurrection of Christ (Rom. 6:1-5; Col. 2:12; 2 Tim. 2:11). And when you go down into the water in Christ's name, you are spiritually dying, burying your sins and your former self in the water, and rising out of the water as a new person, just as Christ rose from the grave with all power (Col. 2:10). Christ himself was baptized by John the Baptist who had already baptized a multitude of people while they confessed their sins to God (Matt. 3). Peter and the apostles baptized three thousand people in one day (Matt. 3:1-11; Acts 2:36-47). Some preachers say baptism places too much emphasis on ceremonial means, and those preachers usually have very large congregations and simply do not want to get in the water to baptize a lot of people every week. But Peter performed the very first baptism after the resurrection of Jesus, and he patiently baptized about three thousand people in one day (Acts 2:36-41). Peter may have had help, but three thousand were baptized. In Acts 10:40-48, the people believed and were filled with the Holy

Ghost, but Peter still commanded them to be baptized in the name of the Lord. The scripture states, "Can anyone object to them being baptized in water and receiving the Holy Ghost, like we have?" (Acts 10:47–48). Yes, the Bible does say, "Whosoever believes in Jesus shall receive forgiveness of sins" (Acts 10:43).

Paul met a group of Christians who believed but had not been baptized, nor did they have the Holy Ghost. Paul then baptized them in the name of Jesus, and they were filled with the Holy Ghost (Acts 19:1–6). Paul himself was told to call on the name of the Lord, but he was also told to be baptized (Acts 22:16). The Apostle Paul said that people who call on the name of Christ should also be sanctified, (1 Cor.1:2). And to be sanctified is to be set aside for holy use by God and to be separated from worldly matters (John 17:17–19; Isa. 29:23; Heb. 2:11; 11:16; 1 Thess. 4:3–8; 5:19–23).

A man in the Bible believed that Jesus is the Son of God and the man himself said, "Here is water. What prevents me from being baptized?" The scripture states, "Philip said, 'If you believe with all your heart, you should be baptized.' And he answered and said, 'I believe that Jesus Christ is the Son of God,' and they both went down into the water, and Philip baptized him" (Acts 8:36–38). A prison guard was told by Paul and Silas to believe, and he and his family shall be saved, but that same family was also baptized in the name of the Lord Jesus Christ, just like all the original apostles were baptized (Acts 2:36–41; 8:14–17; 10:42–48; 16:25–34; 19:2–5; John 3:3–7).

If a preacher is telling you that obeying only Rom. 10:9–13 will save you, they are lacking wisdom, or they are a lying false prophet. Some preachers stand in the presence of thousands and thousands of people and even more thousands on television and on the Internet and tell them, "Raise your hands and repeat after me." After they recite Romans 10:9, the preacher then tells the people that they are saved, born-again, part of the body of Christ, and on their way to heaven. That is not true, and it is best for a person to voluntarily give their life to Christ and to recite those scriptures and not repeat what a minister says who does not know if the person means what they say or not. We must openly confess Christ and believe in him before and after baptism. They who believe and are baptized shall be saved, but they who do not believe shall be damned (Mark 16:16; Rev. 21:8, 27; 22:14–15).

So obviously, if you believe, you must also get baptized (Mark 16:16). If you believe and do not confess and repent, you may go to hell (Mark 8:38; Matt. 10:32–33; Acts 17:26, 29–31).

Simply confessing and believing will not save you, because repentance and proper baptism is also required. Notice that all the people in the Bible were baptized in the name of Jesus and not in the name of the Father, and of the Son, and of the Holy Ghost (Acts 2:36–44; 8:14–17; 10:40–48; 19:1–6; John 3:3–7).

The Bible says we must live by every Word of God and not just by the part that says that we are saved when we believe, confess, call on God, and are baptized in the name of the Father, and of the Son, and of the Holy Ghost (Luke 4:4; Exod. 24:7; Deut. 4:1–9; 8:3). Those scriptures are in the Bible, but so are thousands of other scriptures, including the ones that say we must live right and that we must be baptized in the name of Christ like the apostles were baptized (Acts 2:36–41; 8:14–17; 10:42–48; 19:2–5; John 3:3–7).

No one can truly confess Jesus but by the Holy Ghost (1 Cor. 12:3). Jesus also says they who believe in him shall receive the Holy Ghost (John 7:37–39). But in Acts 5:32, when the Holy Ghost had been given to the apostles, they said Jesus shall give the Holy Ghost to people who obey Christ. "'Christ the Redeemer shall come to people who turn from sin,' says the Lord" (Acts 5:32; Luke 11:13; John 14:13-18, 26-27; Heb. 5:7-9; Isa. 59:20).

So, as you can see, to "believe" means to "obey" Jesus and live a sanctified life (John 17:17–19; Isa. 29:23). People who sin are of the devil because sin is of the devil and not of God (1 John 3:8–10; John 8:34–47; 1 Tim. 5:15).

We must be separated from willful sin (Heb. 10:26; 4:14–16; Mic. 2:1; Ps. 19:12–14; Rom. 1:18–32; 2 Thess. 2:10–15).

The Bible says that at the very first baptism, the people believed, had all things in common, and were baptized in the name of Jesus (Acts 2:36–44). If any preacher tells you that simply believing and confessing will save you, they are limited in wisdom, or they are a lying false prophet or a hypocrite preacher. Rom. 10:10 tells us to believe unto righteousness and to confess unto salvation, just as 2 Cor. 7:10 says that we should repent unto salvation, or we will die.

The Bible says that God will speak peace to his people, but they must not turn again to folly (Ps. 85:8; 2 Cor. 7:10). Again, the Bible also says that the Lord knows people who are his and let everyone who confesses the name of Christ depart from sin (2 Tim. 2:19; James 2:7). Flee youthful lusts and follow righteousness, faith, love, and peace with people who call on the Lord with a pure heart, daily (2 Tim. 2:22; Job 27:8–23; Ps. 1; Prov. 3:5–8).

Luke 1:50 says God's mercy is on people who fear him. Hezekiah walked before the Lord in truth and with a perfect heart and did that which was good in the sight of God (2 Kings 20:3). David asked God to cleanse his "heart" from willful, unwilful, and unknown sins so he will be acceptable in the sight of the Lord (Ps. 19:12–14). The Lord's eyes run to and from throughout the earth; to show himself strong on behalf of people whose heart is perfect toward him (2 Chron. 16:9). And God knows that Satan works hard against strong Christians who obey God's Word and who live and suffer like Christ (Rev. 12:17).

Josiah and Hezekiah were the two most righteous kings in the Bible, second and third behind King Jesus (2 Kings 18:4–7; 23:25). Josiah turned unto the Lord with all his heart, soul, and might (2 Kings 23:25). In the New Testament, Christ also commands us to serve the Lord with all our heart, soul, and mind (Matt. 22:37). Just as God's eyes searches the earth for people who serve him with a perfect heart so he can be strong for them, the devil roams the earth like an angry lion seeking to devour weak Christians and anti-Christians (1 Pet. 5:8). As state earlier, a certain woman in the Bible told Jesus, "Blessed is the womb that bore you, and the breast that you sucked." Jesus replied, "Blessed are they who obey the Word of God" (Luke

11:27–28). Jesus says that anyone who obeys his Word shall never die (John 8:51).

Hypocrite preachers tell the people what their itching ears want to hear, while the preacher denies God who called them, and the truth shall be evil spoken of by the congregation (2 Tim. 4:2–3; Prov. 17:3–4; 2 Pet. 2:1–2). They will be punished along with the false prophet (Ezek. 14:10; Jer. 23:34–39; Hosea 4:9). And the hypocrite teacher will certainly bear the judgment of God (Gal. 5:7–10).

If people are going to live by the part of the Bible that says we are saved when we believe and confess, then they should obey the rest of the scripture as well. They should obey the part that says we must live by God's righteousness and not our own (Rom. 10:1–3, 9–10). To believe is to have faith, but faith without works is dead, and faith without works cannot save you (James 2:13–26; Matt. 7:7; Mark 2:1–5). Paul said, "According to the faith of God's elect people, and the acknowledging of the truth which is after godliness" (Titus 1:1). To acknowledge means to confess, accept, or admit the truth of. Again, Jesus says, "People draw near unto me with their mouth, and honor me with their lips, but their heart is far from me. In vain do they worship me, teaching for doctrines the commandments of humans" (Mark 7:6–7; Col. 2:22; Titus 1:14; Jer. 12:2; Ezek. 33:31; John 7:18; 1 John 3:18; 1 Thess. 2:4–6, 13).

They disregard God's Word and live by the statutes that they made (2 Kings 17:19; Ps. 28:4–5). Isaiah also said the same thing in the Old Testament (Isa. 29:13; Eph. 4:14; 1 Cor. 1:10; 2:9–16; Rom. 15:5–6).

The book of Malachi says, "You have wearied the Lord with your words. Yet you say, how have we wearied him? When you say people who do evil are good in the sight of the Lord," (Mal. 2:17). Jesus is the savior of all people, especially of those who truly believe (1 Tim. 4:10).

To the pure, God will show himself pure, but to the sinful, he will show himself as a punishing judge (2 Sam. 22:27; Ps. 18:26). Blessed are the pure in heart, for they shall see God (Matt. 5:8).

The commandment of the Lord is pure, rejoicing the heart and enlightening the eyes (Ps. 19:8). The Bible says that whoever shall call on the name of the Lord shall be saved (Joel 2:32; Acts 2:21; Rom. 10:13). This is true, but you must be trying to live a holy and sanctified life as well. When the Bible says that whoever shall call on the name of the Lord shall be saved, that scripture is written in the same chapter of the Bible as the scripture that says that we must be baptized in the name of the Lord Jesus Christ and receive the gift of the Holy Ghost (Acts 2:21, 36 – 44; John 3:3 – 5). So, we must delight in the Lord and call on him always, not just in times of need (Job 27:8–23; Prov. 3:5–8).

False preachers, false prophets, and lying preachers are abusing and misusing the scriptures that say we are saved when we confess and believe, and it is getting worse and worse. Gospel musician Kirk Franklin said on his radio show in 2016 that people can consider their house clean because they listened to his radio show play music. That was one of the biggest lies ever told by a musician. God told Hezekiah to get his house in order because his death was near, but Hezekiah repented in tears, humility, and in fear of God and as a result he lived fifteen more years (Isa. 38). We also must take heed to the whole Word of God (Luke 4:4; Exod. 24:7; Deut. 4:1–9; 8:3). We must not live by the commandments of mankind as with Kirk Franklin's false statement (Mark 7:6–7; Col. 2:22; Eph. 4:14; 1 Cor. 1:10; 2:9–16; Rom. 15:5–6).

People who live by Kirk Franklin's words and the words of false prophets and lying preachers disregard God's Word and live by the statutes that humans made (2 Kings 17:19; Ps. 28:4–5).

People who believe that all they must do to be saved is to confess with their mouth and believe in their heart are making mention of God's name, but not in truth nor in righteousness (Isa. 48:1; Rom. 10:9–10, 13; Heb. 6:1–6). The Bible also says that we must not simply believe in our heart, but that we must praise the Lord with uprightness of heart, while we learn God's righteous judgments (Ps. 119:7). It is time to awake out of sinful sleep, spiritually lazy sleep, and acts of omission toward God because our salvation and our judgment day are closer than when we first believed. "The night is far spent, the day is at hand, let us therefore cast off works of darkness, and let us put on the armor of light. Let us walk honestly, as in the day, not in partying, drunkenness, sexual sins, evil conduct, fighting, and jealousy. Instead, put on the Lord Jesus Christ, and make no provisions for the flesh, to fulfill lusts" (Rom. 13:11–13; Gal. 5:13). For most people, judgment day is the day that they die and not on the last day when God destroys the earth (Rev. 22:10–13; Acts 24:15; 1 Pet. 3:18; Dan. 12:1–3; Ezek. 18:19–32; 2 Thess. 1:4–12).

There is a book of our works being recorded in heaven, and God judges us based on what is in the Book of Works, and that determines if he writes our name in the Book of Life in heaven forever (Rev. 3:1–6; 20:12–13; Phil. 4:3; Mal. 3:16).

Believing and confessing are only the first steps (Rom. 10:9, 13). Those scriptures sometimes refer to various situations in life, mainly people who are sick and bedridden and cannot be baptized due to their illness and any other person who cannot get to a body of water such as some prison inmates and when people would like to give their life to Christ and are making plans to be baptized in the very near future. In defense of Romans 10:9 that says we are saved when we simply believe, confess, and call on the name of the Lord, Peter said the same thing in Acts 10:42–48; but Peter also said in those same scriptures that we must be baptized in the name of Jesus Christ and receive the gift of the Holy Ghost (Acts 2:36–44; 8:14–17; 10:40–48; 19:1–6; John 3:3–7).

BLESSINGS DO NOT ALWAYS MEAN THAT A PERSON IS SAVED

Before Jesus died, rose from the dead, and ascended back to heaven, he only ministered to the ancient Jews. Christ sent Paul to the Gentiles, and God told Peter to accept the Gentiles, but that was after Christ went back to heaven. Before that time, an unsaved woman approached Jesus and asked that he heal her daughter. Jesus told her that he did not come to minister to people who were not of the ancient Jews, and why should he take from God's children and give to dogs? The woman told Jesus that even dogs eat of the crumbs that fall from the children's table. At that point, Jesus granted her request (Matt. 15:21–28). As you can see, just because a sinner receives things from God, that does not mean that God is pleased with them, and it does not mean that sinners are saved. Now that Christ is calling all people to repentance, why wouldn't he bless sinners (Acts 17:26, 29–31)? Do you give only to your most obedient child and not give to the disobedient child occasionally? The child who is more obedient to God and to parents should receive the most and on a more regular basis, but you cannot totally disregard the disobedient child. You must give them things at times to show them that you love them, but that does not mean that you are pleased with their disobedience. Therefore, God's blessings shine on the just and the unjust, the good, the evil, and the unthankful but that does not mean that unthankful and unjust people are going to heaven (Deut. 9:4–7; 10:17–22; Ezek. 29:17–20; Matt. 5:43–48;

Luke 6:35; Acts 14:8–18; Ps. 17:13–15; Neh. 9:35–39; Ps. 145:9–10).

OBEYING ONLY THREE VERSES OF THE BIBLE DOES NOT SAVE YOU

When people say that "all you have to do to be saved is to believe," they are like lazy people who have a new job and say all they must do is a little work. We should not look for the least amount of anything regarding God, and to do our very best towards God is our reasonable service, while also being a holy living sacrifice unto Christ (Rom. 12:1; Luke 17:7-10). And obedience is better than sacrifice, because God desires righteousness towards him and mankind, and mercy towards other people more than he desires sacrifice (1 Sam. 15:22; Rom. 12:1 – 2; Matt. 9:10 – 13; 23:23; Prov. 21:3; Ps. 4:5; 40:6 – 8: Hos. 6:6; Mic. 6:7; Heb. 13:15).

Even if we cannot live up to all of God's high standards and high expectations, the Lord still has very high standards and expectations, not low ones (Heb. 4:12; Rev. 1:16; 2:12, 16; 19:13; Matt. 10:34-39; 1 John 5:12; Eph. 6:17; John 1:1).

Why should we expect to do little obedience toward God but receive plenty of blessings from God? We are supposed to be servants of the Lord, and he is not our servant. God should not have to continue to wait on us, and wait for us, and to give us everything we need while we do little toward him. Obedience is better than sacrifice and is our minimum service and requirement (1 Sam. 15:22; Rom. 12:1 – 2; Matt. 9:10 – 13; 23:23; Prov. 21:3; Ps. 4:5; 40:6 – 8: Hos. 6:6; Mic. 6:7; Heb. 13:15).

CONFESSING WITH YOUR MOUTH, BELIEVING IN YOUR HEART

    The Bible says that God requires all people everywhere, in every nation, to repent and turn away from their sins and God shall judge the world in righteousness on judgment day (Luke 24:46–49; Acts 14:8–18; 17:26, 29–31). Therefore, it is a terrible lie when people say that all you must do to be saved is to believe, confess, and call on the name of the Lord (Rom. 10:9, 13).

    Some Protestants claim that Catholics are not aligned with the Bible, especially when Catholics go before a priest to confess their sins and to ask for forgiveness as though the priest is God. But when Protestant preachers stand before multitudes of people and tell them that they are saved after they simply recite Romans 10:9–10, 13, they mislead millions of people yearly. God says in the Old Testament and Christ says in the New Testament that we must live by every Word of God (Luke 4:4; Exod. 24:7; Deut. 4:1–9; 8:3). This does not mean that we are able to obey all of it, but we must acknowledge, stand for, and live by all of it while confessing that we must not live in or support sin. Jesus says that he wishes people were cold or hot, because if we are lukewarm, he spits us out of his mouth. God chastises people who he loves, and they must repent and turn away from their sins or they will be lost in their sins to the grave and to hell. Because people who obey sin are servants and slaves of sin, and they are not servants of Christ (Rev. 3:15-19; Rom. 6:15-17).

We must be on fire for the Lord after we confess and believe, otherwise we are cold and lost. Christ seeks us to save us but to only confess, believe, and call on him in times of need is to be lukewarm, and God rejects and spits out lukewarm people. Jesus also says, "Either make the tree good and its fruit good, or make the tree bad and its fruit bad, because a tree is known by the fruit it produces" (Matt. 12:33). Even a child is known by their ways, whether they are pure or right (Prov. 20:11). "Blessed are they who hunger and thirst for righteousness, for they shall be filled" (Matt. 5:6; Ps. 42:1-3; Prov. 15:8-9; Rev. 21:6-8; 22:13-21).

Some people make themselves rich but have nothing because they are empty, blind, miserable, and unsaved; but some poor people are rich with salvation, sanctification, holiness, happiness, good health, good children, peace, wisdom, necessities, strength, safety, and protection (Prov. 13:7; Rev. 3:15-22). Some of God's people live like Christ lived on earth, in tribulation and poverty, but are still rich (Rev. 2:9). God fills hungry people with good things, but he sends ungodly rich people away empty (Luke 1:53). Notice that the scripture did not say that hungry people are filled with food, but with good things, whatever those things may be. God fills people who hunger with whatever good thing their soul hungers for, but sometimes we must seek God and not simply wait on him to show up—seek and you shall find (Luke 11:9-10; Matt. 11:28-30; Jer. 6:16). Rebellious people shall seek but not find, and they shall call on God, but he will not answer, because they did not choose the fear of the Lord (Luke 6:25; Prov. 1:28-30). In the Old Testament, God says that the sins of some people are written upon the tables of their heart with an iron diamond-tipped pen (Jer. 17:1). But God is asking us to write his Word in our hearts and minds (Prov. 3:3; Jer. 31:33; 2 Cor. 3:2-3, 7).

Everyone who forsakes the Lord shall be ashamed, and they who depart from the Lord shall be written in the earth, meaning in the grave and not written in the Book of Life, because they have forsook the Lord, who is the fountain of living water (Jer.

17:13; John 7:37–39; Rev. 22:18–19; Rom. 1:24–25; Deut. 4:2; 5:22; 12:32; Ezra 6:11; Prov. 30:5–6; Eccles. 3:14–15).

BONUS READING

CORONAVIRUS (COVID-19)

In March of 2020, there was a global outbreak of Coronavirus (also called COVID-19). It may have happened because many people, including some Christians accepted; embraced; and supported homosexuality, abortions, and late-term abortions. We do know that those abominations, murders, and evil, wicked sins were legalized on a global scale; and only a few years later, there was a global outbreak of Coronavirus, which was something the world had never seen or heard of before, just as global and worldwide acceptance of anti-God practices were legalized globally like never before.

We do know that God promises to not allow disease, affliction, and adversity in our lands when we obey his Word; and that if we do not obey his Word, God says he allows prolonged disease and sickness in the land and even new diseases and illnesses that are not written in the Bible (Exod. 15:26; Deut. 7:12–15; 28:58–61; Rev. 2:18–29; Rom. 5:9; Jer. 30:12–15; Ps. 38; 107:17). Most pandemics and natural disasters are a result of God being displeased with our sinful actions. Many people live by laws and practices that they made or supported; and that results in pain, natural disasters, bad weather, sorrow, sickness, disease, death, and destruction (2 Kings 17:19; Ps. 28:4–5).

Most people did not acquire the Coronavirus. God is too gracious and merciful to allow that to happen. But he does have a way of getting everyone's attention, instilling fear in everyone, and causing almost everyone to pray unto him, but some people are too hard-hearted to pray. God punishes people harder who do not take heed to his rebuke and warnings and who do not choose the fear of the Lord (Prov. 1:28–30). The Lord will take sickness out of the land when people turn again to him, confess his name in righteousness, pray, repent and turn away from their rebellion (Exod. 23:25; Deut. 7:15; 28; 29:2–6; 2 Chron. 7:14; Matt. 13:14–15; Luke 19:37–42; Isa. 6:8–10; Lev. 20:6–27; Jer. 4:22).

We should not be surprised when we see and hear of new diseases, destruction, and death because the Bible says that in these last days, dangerous and perilous times will continue to happen due to sin, hypocrisy, blasphemy, and rebellion and that our generation will experience more tribulation and trouble than the world has ever known or will ever hear of again. Because most people do not accept the love of the truth of God's Word (Matt. 24:21; Mark 13:19; Dan. 12:1; 2 Thess. 2; 1 Tim. 4:1–3; Mic. 5:2, 4, 15).

The last days for most of us are the days before we die because most people will not live to see the last day of the earth's existence (2 Tim. 3:1–7; 1 John 2:18). But God allows most of us to die sooner or later because most of us must die to get to heaven unless we are alive on the last day of the earth's existence. Saved people who are alive on the last day of the earth's existence will be instantly transformed into angels without ever dying (1 Thess. 4:13–18; 1 John 2:18).

Not everyone who died from COVID-19 is going to hell and not everyone who died from COVID-19 was an enemy of God. But people who support worldly anti-God laws, practices, and policies are enemies of God (James 4:4; John 1:10–12; 15:18–19; 1 John 2:15–17; 3:13; Phil. 3:16–21).

If anyone thinks that COVID-19 had nothing to do with mankind legalizing homosexual marriages and abortions, including late-term abortions, then do they think that God will never punish the world for that level of rebellion, blasphemy, and hypocrisy? God says, "Shall I not visit the earth for these sins?" (Prov. 19:23; Jer. 5:9, 29; 14:10). Sin separates us from our God (Isa. 1:15; 59:1–2; 64:4–8; Ps. 107:17–22; Mal. 2:2).

Some humans try to void God's Word, and that causes God to have a controversy with the inhabitants of the land and causes humans to not be able to go to work so God can work (Ps. 119:126; Job 37:7; Hos. 4:1–2). And if COVID-19 is not one of God's ways of punishing the world for embracing abortions and homosexuality, that only means that harder times are coming because God shall act regarding abortions and homosexuality. And Christ says that the tribulations, troubles, and diseases that we suffer are only the beginning of sorrows (Matt. 24:3–8). Some of those sorrows have come to past already during times like World War I and World War II, but the Bible says that times will be harder and harder, and that trouble in our generations are only the beginning of sorrows (Matt. 24:3–8). God's Word will never return to him void. God eventually does exactly what he says he will do, whether he promises to send blessings or death and destruction (Isa. 14:24; 46:9–10; 55:10–11; Jer. 23:20; Ezek. 5:13; 6:9–10; 12:21–28; 22:14; 24:13–14; Dan. 9:12–14; Matt. 24:32–44; 2 Pet. 3:6–14; 2 Kings10:10).

Several scientists in April 2020 said that COVID-19 was not man-made, but that it did probably originate in China. Most people know that China was and maybe still is an extremely anti-Christ nation. Therefore, God may have used COVID-19 to punish them although some people believe that China created the virus to decrease their extremely large human population. Hopefully, it was not made by humans on purpose with evil intentions, but if it was made by humans, the Bible says that God made everything, even wicked people, for the day of evil (Prov. 16:2–7; Isa. 45:5–7; Lam. 3:37–40). In other words, God sometimes uses evil inventions to punish people because the inventions are accessible to him, even if he did not create them himself. Those same scriptures also say that people who invent wicked things shall not go unpunished, and by the fear of the Lord, people depart from evil and that when a person's ways and works please the Lord, God makes even their enemies to be at peace with them (Prov.16:2–7).

The government of New York boldly embraced almost every

anti-God law and practice that mankind created, and that is one reason they suffered so much. Louisiana also had a high number of COVID-19 cases, and they suffer a lot in Louisiana from hurricanes, floods, and other forms of adversity because Louisiana is basically the modern-day magic, sorcery, voodoo, and witchcraft capital of the United States. Mardi Gras crowds are believed to be the reason that COVID-19 cases were so high in Louisiana, but Mardi Gras itself is anti-Christian. Mardi Gras originated with pagan and heathen ties and is a time when people make one last effort to indulge in eating, drinking, and sinning before the celebration of the life, crucifixion, death, and resurrection of our Lord and Savior Jesus Christ. Mardi Gras ends on Fat Tuesday, and people have historically repented for their sins the following day on Ash Wednesday, which is the first day of Lent and the beginning of the preparation for Holy Week, Passion Week, Passover week, resurrection week, and Resurrection Day, erroneously called Easter by most people.

The harder people speak and stand against God, the harder his punishment is toward those people (Ps. 90:11; Jude 1:14–25). Therefore, it is no coincidence that American and European nations suffered the most from COVID-19. It is one thing to be a non-Christian, but it is a lot worse to be a hypocrite Christian. At least non-Christians in their nations do not pretend to be Christians, and God says that many so-called Christians are worse than people who do not claim to be Christians (Jer. 2:32–33; 5:28–31; 2 Chron. 33:9; Matt. 5:19; 23:15; 2 Kings 21:10–12; Lam. 4:6; Ezek. 16:47–48; 1 Tim. 5:8; 1 Cor. 5:1).

God says that he will heal the land if people who are called by his name shall pray, repent, and turn from their wicked ways (2 Chron. 7:13 – 14; Isa. 6:8–10; Ezek. 33:31; Matt. 13:14–15; Luke 19:37–42; Deut. 29:2–6). Killing unborn babies and supporting that practice is evil and wicked. Remember, just as our leaders can cause great peace and prosperity in the land, our leaders can also cause God's wrath to strike the land. Just as was the case when the land suffered a great famine during the days of King David. David prayed to God, and God told David that the famine was punishment for the sins of King Saul, who was David's predecessor (2 Sam. 21:1). And it is highly likely that COVID-19 happened because of the wicked abortion and homosexual laws that President Barack Obama and other world leaders legalized.

Noteworthy, after the Lord finally ended the global pandemic, worldwide inflation struck the earth to the point that most people said it sometimes felt and looked like a recession. This happened because many people did not repent and turn to the Lord during the pandemic, even though God spared their life.

REFERENCES

The Holy Ghost, also known as the Holy Spirit

The King James Version of the Holy Bible

ABOUT THE AUTHOR

Elijah Paul

The author Elijah Paul has published six books and is a Christian minister who has been in the ministry since the 1990's. All the author's initial developments of his books began by the direction of God Almighty as part of a much larger book nearly twenty-three years before he published his first book. The Lord showed the author the original vision that caused him to begin writing, and God gave additional visions through the years as the Lord revealed them to the author. The original work was written over a twenty-two-year period and consists of more than 1,400 pages and more than 2,000 topics. The author's original vision from God included a vision of a number 2, which caused the author to assume that the larger book would be published after two years of writing. As years passed, the author became worried that he was not fulfilling God's work and that pursuing advanced college degrees and handling adversities, afflictions, trials, and tribulations were delaying the larger book's completion date. As more years passed, the author assumed that the number 2 that he saw in the vision must have involved the number 12 which is a significant number in the Bible, but after the larger book was still far from being completed after twelve years, the author assumed that the vision of the number 2 must have been twenty years. And after twenty years of writing, the author felt that he had failed to fulfill God's calling and purpose. But when the larger book was finally finished after twenty-two years of writing, the author realized that the number 2 that he saw in the vision was twenty-two years and also the year 2020.

After twenty-two years of writing, God finally revealed to the author that the larger book will never be published as one huge book, but that several smaller books will be published from the original larger book. The first smaller book was taken out of the larger book and published in the year 2020. Therefore, the fulfillment of the vision of the number 2 is twenty-two years to finish writing, and the first book was published in the year 2020. The author Elijah Paul plans to spend the rest of his life publishing books from his twenty-two years of documenting revelations from Christ.

BOOKS BY THIS AUTHOR

Slaveholders, Churches & Colonists Changed The Bible. The Greatest Identity Theft In History. Black Jews & Black Egyptians Changed To White

God Is With You In Hard Times When You Think That He Is Not

The Recrucifixion Of Christ By Barack Obama & Christians Who Support Homosexuality & Abortions (Sold At Walmart.com, Google Play, Apple Books, Barnesandnoble.com, Booksamillion.com, Thriftbooks.com)

Favor Of God, Forgetting Your Past, Remembering Where God Brought You From

One Lord, One Faith, One Baptism, All Your Questions Answered With Scriptures

Crucifixion Of Christ By President Obama

BACK COVER SUMMARY

More and more ministers are falsely teaching that people do not need to be baptized at all to become a born-again Christian. This book peacefully explains with supporting Holy Scriptures how God is One Lord, and that God's plan is for there to be only One Faith, meaning one church. The name of the church does not matter if the church members are on the one foundation of God, and part of the one body of Christ. It is still acceptable to identify a church as, for example, the Methodist Church, the Catholic Church, or the Baptist Church, but there is only one foundation, One Faith, and truthfully One Baptism that is ordained by God Almighty. This book also explains how, "Confessing with Your Mouth, Believing in Your Heart, and Calling on the Name of the Lord" is vital in the life of a Christian, but this is not all that must be done to become a born-again Christian. There is one Bonus Reading titled, "Coronavirus (COVID-19)." This is the fifth book published by the author Elijah Paul and it is a Holy Ghost given guide to becoming a saved, born-again Christian, and a new creation in Christ.

www.ingramcontent.com/pod-product-compliance
Lightning Source LLC
Chambersburg PA
CBHW032133040426
42449CB00005B/224